RISING FROM DECEPTION

DECEPTION

Recovering from an Internet Scam

JANET MARSHALL

RISING FROM DECEPTION
RECOVERING FROM AN INTERNET SCAM

ISBN: 979-8-9858943-0-1 (paperback)
ISBN: 979-8-9858943-1-8 (ebook)

DEDICATION

To my mother, Mary E., who began her writing career long after raising her family. Prior to that, her experience was limited to letter writing with her family and friends. She enrolled in a Creative Writing class at the university at the seasoned age of forty, and has been chronicling her life in enchanting stories ever since. She has been my inspiration to pen my own journey.

TABLE OF CONTENTS

PROLOGUE

I just want a nice boyfriend!

His photo on the dating website captured my interest. I was flattered that he was interested in me. I opened my heart to a man who knew what to say to a lonely widow. It only took a few days and I was hooked on this man.

My loneliness was replaced by virtual companionship, as each day we sent text messages during my morning coffee, an afternoon 'hello', and a treasured 'sweet dreams, my Queen' before I retired at night. We were texting intimate details of our lives. I dreamed of the day we would meet in person.

It was not long before he was in a difficult situation and asked for financial help. By then, I was emotionally captured in his web of deception, and refusing to help him was inconceivable. And that was precisely according to his plan.

My story is an example of how far these people will go to get someone's money, what might motivate a victim to give into their demands, and what I learned about myself through my experience. Many believe they will never fall victim and do such out-of-character things. But this man, this scammer, was too skilled for my naïveté, and I am quite certain, for others as well.

If you are aware of any internet scams please make an FBI report on:
Internet Crime Complaint Center – IC3

1

Part I

OLD WOUNDS

Everyone, if they live long enough, endures some painful moments. We never know what's going on inside somebody—and everyone has something going on inside them. I had my fair share of difficulties, but my faith in God, fortitude, and support system carried me through. Some wounds didn't surface until later in life, but some were deeply impactful.

In Part I, I've included three personal events, from the sixty years prior to my online dating experience. Names and places have been changed to protect the family's privacy.

1: SNOWFLAKES

Giant snowflakes were floating down and landing on my black hair, black coat, and black gloves. It was surreal, standing on a hill looking at the small white casket on the ground in front of me. I was oblivious of the people around me, my parents and sisters, and my husband's family. I couldn't focus on the words my priest was saying. He had a soothing and familiar tone, however. Eight months before, he had said the words, "I now pronounce you man and wife." But instead of focusing on his voice, I noticed how each snowflake on my black coat sleeve was similar, but none were the same.

A few days before, I'd felt my baby move inside me. Feeling the first labor pains that night, caused me to hide under the bedcovers, willing away the fears. I was only twenty-four weeks along in my first pregnancy. Baby Ben was born that night, and lived twenty-five hours. The morning after his brief experience in this unfair world, I held my unmoving son in my arms. I rocked slowly in the chair in that sterile hospital nursery, then finally let him go.

The funeral director's wife went to Kmart. She bought a doll outfit to dress my two-pound, two-ounce baby boy to allow our family to view him before being placed in the cold, dark hole in the ground.

After the funeral, I lost myself for awhile. I crawled into grief and cocooned it around me, unable to care about anything. Eventually, I had to emerge from hibernation. Poking my head out the door, hearing the spring birds singing, and feeling the sun on my face, I forced myself to participate in activities again.

In the next ten years, while living in a 1000 square foot house, we had four girls, and one boy, all before I was thirty years old. I loved teaching my children how to follow along with me as I read the same story repeatedly. I was exhausted almost every night, but content. Ray worked the afternoon shift, from 3:00 p.m. till 11:30 p.m., so he was absent during the evening hours.

We bought some property and built a 2000 square foot home on it with four bedrooms. It was double the size of our first home. I knew our family would thrive nicely out there. We had two children in the next five years, both boys, which made the grand total seven.

I can't believe I raised twenty-five chickens from day-old chicks. We weren't farmers but gave it a try. The deal at the feed store was if one purchased a twenty-five-pound bag of chick feed, you would receive twenty-five chicks FREE. My goal was to provide a hands-on lesson for the kids, teaching them where their food came from, and to lower the grocery budget for this family of nine. How could they determine the sex of a chick only a few days old? They were all roosters! We raised them until they were big enough to eat. Learning from a library book, I was able to skin and cut up these fellas. They went into the stew pot or I froze them. Not a drumstick was wasted.

***

Early one mild May evening, I was reclining on the couch after a full day at school, where I worked. We'd been married thirty years. My eyes were closed, but I wasn't sleeping when the house phone rang.

The caller asked, "Is this Mrs. Marshall, and do you have a son, Roger?"

"Yes."

"I am the doctor treating your son at St. Andrew's Hospital. He was brought here by ambulance a few minutes ago. He's unconscious. He was riding his bicycle and fell or maybe passed out. A man and woman walking down the sidewalk called 911. His backpack contained a change of clothes, a roll of toilet paper, a journal and several bottles of prescription medication. I haven't determined what's going on with him yet. Do you think he could have drunk antifreeze?" the doctor asked.

I had no idea how to answer this question. Drink car antifreeze? Why? Roger, twenty-three years old, lived in his own apartment, but I hadn't talked to him yet, as I did most days. Had I been there recently to visit him, I would have seen the empty fifth of vodka in the garbage and the almost empty gallon jug of vehicle antifreeze on the kitchen counter.

Roger had been dealing with depression and that spring was placed on academic probation in his third year at Eastern Michigan University. I found it hard to breathe on this frightening drive to the hospital as I anticipated the worst.

Upon entering the ER I saw my son lying, almost naked, on a hospital bed in that cold room. His head was lying to the side, his eyes closed and mouth open, and he looked dead. I grabbed Roger, held him tight, and sobbed violently. Had I lost my tender-hearted son?

Over the next eleven days, Roger remained in the ICU unconscious. I stayed the first night, sleeping on an uncomfortable sofa in the family waiting room. I was allowed to visit him for the first ten minutes of every hour, but woke up abruptly the morning after the first night, not sure where I was.

"Mommy, is that lady dead?"

Opening my eyes, trying to focus to determine where I was, a cute little girl stood next to me. Her shocked mother stood behind her. They had come to the hospital early this morning to get blood drawn. The room I slept in was also used for those waiting for their laboratory procedures. Throughout the night it was mostly vacant, but started to fill up again early in the morning, with people waiting to get their lab work done.

"I'm not dead," I said, "but I think I need a brush to fix my hair." I cautiously sat up on the couch and began folding up the hospital-issued blanket. "Can you help me fold this?" I said.

She smiled, and like innocent, nonjudgmental children often do, right away was my helper to straighten up the whole room.

My son started to awaken on day twelve, but we feared he would have some permanent brain damage or possible nerve damage, so we were very anxious. He had undergone several days of kidney dialysis to clean his system of the poison he had ingested. Roger was a young, otherwise healthy twenty-three-year-old. We learned his diagnosis, schizophrenia often erupted in one's early twenties. This disease was incurable but could be controlled with intensive therapy and a monitored medication regimen. We are so grateful for the chance to be with him again.

2: ONE STAR

"Mom, Will you pray with me?" my youngest son Jerry asked as he came into the family room where I was reading. I looked up and saw the frightened look on his face. He was sixteen years old.

"I found out my friend has tried to kill herself by taking a whole lot of pills. She called me just before she did it. Nothing I said convinced her not to do it." I immediately starting calling local hospitals. We both let out a huge sigh of relief when her mother called Jerry to tell him she'd found her daughter in time, and had gotten her to the hospital.

I got my prayer book out and found a few prayers I thought appropriate for this situation. I couldn't think straight to recite any from memory, nor could I compose anything on the spot. I found the *St. Anthony Litany* and began reading, "From all hardness of heart, from fear, anger and strife, from every injustice." Jerry's response was, "St. Anthony, pray for us." Afterward, I realized my son had taught me a precious lesson. Don't panic, just PRAY. I was blessed to be the mother of this resilient and faith filled young man.

***

Jerry, the youngest of my seven children, enjoyed a successful high school football career and was popular with his friends, but he struggled to find his place in the adult world. After high-school he attended one semester of community college, and decided it was not for him. He was a hard worker. His dad taught him how to dig trenches, apply asphalt sealer, and to take care of his own car repairs. Jerry's hard work at home and on the ball field would prepare him for his chosen career.

He made the decision on his own, and enlisted in the Army shortly after his twenty-first birthday. His dad wasn't sure it was the best for his son, as in 2006, the war in Iraq was intense. There were casualties almost every week. But Jerry informed us he would probably be deployed to Afghanistan. We were relieved he wasn't going to Iraq.

We were all proud of Jerry's commitment to make a difference in our country. His letters and phone calls revealed a mature and happy young man. He loved basic training. In fact, he said he'd like to do it again, it was so fun and so much like football practice. After military graduation, but before returning to Ft. Benning, Georgia for further training he suggested we all go to our northern Michigan cabin for a short family vacation. Jerry's attitude was buoyant and we followed his lead.

It was a cold, rainy April weekend, but we had a bonfire outside, cooked lots of food, and laughed at each other's stories of family trips of long ago. His brother-in-law made a tent over the fire pit, so a group of them could hang out there like they'd always done. I remember washing dishes in the kitchen at about 11:00 p.m. as Jerry was sitting on the barstool nearby. Under the influence of a few Heinekins, he began sharing some personal experiences of his teenage life and time during basic training. Our cabin was small, so the sisters and their families slept on the floor or couches in the adjoining family room. I held back laughter as Jerry told me personal tales about his first sexual experience when he was sixteen, and of how some of the guys in basic training would do funny things with their "johnsons." He was being serious. Maybe some of the family "sleeping" nearby heard him as well.

***

Vicenza, Italy, was Jerry's home for the next two months in Camp Ederle, where the 173rd Army Airborne Infantry brigade was based. Early in May 2007, Jerry was among the one hundred men of the 173rd Airborne Brigade airdropped into a remote area of Kunar Province, in northern Afghanistan. Their units patrolled the small villages nearby, becoming familiar with the area and the people. This was Taliban territory, deep within the Hindu Kush Mountains and near the suspected hideout of Osama bin Laden. In one letter to the family, Jerry wrote about handing out candy he received in a care package from his sister, Sam. He told of instructing the village kids to stand in a line, and he gave the girls their candy first. His letter described his frustration about the boys treating the girls rudely. The adult males were the same with their wives, he said. Rude, crude and mostly used them to procreate.

The afternoon of July 5, 2007, the day after an Independence Day celebration with our family, a knock came at our front door. I opened it to see two uniformed soldiers, adorned with many impressive medals on their jackets, staring at me. My heart sank. I stood there frozen in the doorway with a blank look on my face. There was no question of the purpose of this visit.

"Mr. and Mrs. Marshall, we represent the United States Army. May we come inside?" After we were all seated around our dining room table one man spoke. "We wish to express our deepest regret that your son, Jerry was killed in action in Kunar Province, Afghanistan early in the day on July 5, 2007. He was killed from wounds sustained from hostile enemy fire.

My husband, Ray pulled Jerry's high school graduation photo down from the wall and sat it on the table. He said, "This is Jerry and I just want you to see who you're talking about." I went into the kitchen and got some beverages from the refrigerator and brought them to the table. "Would you like anything to drink?" I said.

"No thank you, Ma'am. This is all the information we have at this time. A Casualty Assistance Officer will reach out to you in person this afternoon, and will guide you in the process of bringing your son home. Again, please accept our gratitude for your son's ultimate sacrifice and our condolences to your entire family."

Our brave son had been in an ambush and was killed from small arms fire. He'd been in the country just thirty days. We received phone calls from his superiors, and they all said Jerry was an exemplary soldier and because of his actions that day, many were able to get out alive. Our son was awarded the Bronze Star and Purple Heart posthumously.

Sgt. James P. would accompany Jerry's body the entire trip from Afghanistan to Waterford, Michigan, which would take almost three days. When the white Angel Flight airplane landed on Detroit's Selfridge Base tarmac, Sgt. James was the first to appear at the door, standing at attention as the casket was rolled out. Our family stood outside the plane, the wind blowing through our hair on this fair July day. His casket draped in the American Flag was wheeled to the funeral hearse waiting nearby. Sgt. Adrian S., our Casualty Assistance Officer would support us through the next days. The Army takes care of the fallen and their families.

The drive from the base to the funeral home was about a thirty-mile ride. I rode with my husband and my parents in the first black limousine following the hearse, and other family members followed in their own cars. Alongside the road were dozens of police, firemen, and other first responders. The officials' cars were parked at an angle on the highway's side, with the occupants standing in front saluting as we drove by. As we passed each city and town along the interstate, we witnessed the same thing. Fire trucks, dump trucks, and police cars assembled on the side of the highway, and the officers saluting their hero coming home. I tried not to miss any of these sights, and held my breath as I squeezed back tears. I felt proud of my son's bravery, lucky to have had a close relationship with him over his twenty-two years, and knew he was already in heaven.

We received visitors at the funeral home for two days. The funeral was at our local church, the same one where Jerry had accompanied me many times. After the funeral Mass, the cemetery procession was several miles long and included over 1000 cars and military Patriot Motorcycle Riders.

I felt honored and proud to have the seventh and eighth grade students from my school participate in the Mass. It had taken me ten years to get my elementary teaching degree attending part time. I walked into my first college class when I was thirty eight years old. During my thirteen years I taught grades one through five, middle school history, and was assistant principal for six years. These kids supported my family and demonstrated how to carry out what they had learned in class: console the downhearted, bury the dead, respect your elders.

Now I had two boys in heaven, my first and last child. I'd used the lesson learned from Jerry to grieve his death. Prayer is powerful.

***

One woman who shared her condolences at the funeral home said she'd started sending care packages to the deployed military in Iraq after the 911 attack on the Twin Towers. When she called me some days later, Laura stated she wanted to name the care packages she was sending overseas in honor of our son. Would we allow it and give our permission? We said YES. So, volunteer patriots, school kids, and old veterans packed and mailed care packages to the deployed military and still do. Another local woman Connie had an idea for a project too. Her father had recently passed away. He was an Air Force veteran and had spent many days in veteran's hospitals. She was also an avid quilter and thought a colorful homemade quilt given to these men would ease their pain. She wanted to name them in honor of our son. We quickly agreed to support her project. I was pleased to join her one year as she delivered quilts to injured military men and women rehabilitating in Walter Reid Hospital in Washington, D.C.

Our family established a college scholarship in Jerry's name, awarded to a high school senior from his school. We asked the students to submit an essay on "What does team mean to you," and our family conducted interviews to determine the recipient. It was heartwarming to ask these young people questions and learn about their future plans. It was another memorable way to honor our son and to preserve his memory.

***

One August 27, 2021, I was stunned to hear that two explosions ripped through crowds outside the Kabul airport, killing and wounding those seeking evacuation from Afghanistan. More than 100 people were killed, including at least 13 U.S. service members and 90 Afghans. The people were trying to enter that American-controlled airport to evacuate the country following the twenty-year war.

As I listened to the news reports of the failed evacuation of Americans stranded in Afghanistan, I felt sickened. I was extremely sad for the loss of more lives. We'd already sacrificed thousands of our best and brightest young people over the last twenty years, in an effort to help Afghanistan better the lives of their people. I was pleased our military was coming home. Let the Afghans figure it out on their own now. Our military was successful in that we haven't had a terrorist attack on our own soil since 9-11-2001. And I was proud of my son for his sacrifice in making that a reality.

3: VACATION IT WAS NOT

February 2014

"Happy Valentine's Day Jan," Ray said when I answered the house phone on Friday, February 14th.

"Happy Valentine's Day to you too. How was your day?"

"I rode the bike into town, stopped at a little shop and talked to the clerks there. They were nice and friendly. But I think I went eight miles, and then I had to ride back to the house again. I'm really tired. I'll fix a snack and then go to bed. I can't wait for you to get here."

"Yes, I'm wrapping things up at school and will leave on Monday morning. Lynn is driving me to the airport in Detroit, so at the end of the month I'll be able to ride back to Michigan with you. We should have almost two weeks together. You won't forget to pick me up at the Tampa airport, will you?"

"No, I'll be there. Good night, Honey. See you on Monday."

"Good night."

I waited at the airport for Ray to pick me up for our vacation together. I didn't see him right away, and got a sinking feeling. I hadn't heard from him since Valentine's Day, three days before. I'd been so busy preparing, I didn't realize this until I was comfortably seated on the plane.

Dear Lord, please help me. I can't take another loss. I'm strong but I have limits. There's something wrong. I know it. I should have heard from him.

In the last ten years of our marriage, our routines had changed. Ray was retired from General Motors and wanted to explore, visit the children and grandchildren, put some miles on his new GMC truck, and keep up with his exercise routine. I was exercising my brain and training teachers at the university. Our times together were limited.

That seventeenth day in February, I waited with my suitcase on the bench outside the Tampa airport, enjoying the warm Florida weather. After an hour and no answer from my repeated calls to Ray's cell phone, I got concerned. *Maybe his cell phone battery has died. Perhaps he had the wrong day written on his calendar. Perhaps he has fallen asleep? Maybe he's here someplace and I can't see him.* Finally, I gave in when I couldn't reach him, and arranged a taxi for the one hour trip to the house. My daughter Sam called me on the cell phone. After I told her the situation, she suggested we have the local police do a welfare check at the rental house. Then she stayed on the phone with me, chatting about what I don't remember. My head was pounding and all kinds of scenarios went through my mind. *What's his deal? Why can't he follow through on a plan? What's the worst that could've happened?*

The taxi driver struggled to find the correct house, making wrong turns here and there, retracing his route according to the GPS.

Sam questioned me, "Where are you now?"

"We're in the right neighborhood, but the driver's still looking for the house."

"Mom, the police went into the house and found Dad dead. They said: "Don't let your mother get out of the taxi.""

I was totally silent in the back seat. Time felt like it stood still. The local police had broken into the locked house and found Ray dead in his bed, apparently a couple of days already. They reported he was lying comfortably in the bed, and it looked like he'd just fallen asleep. I learned

Ray had passed away probably that day we had last talked, Valentine's Day. He'd suffered a massive heart attack.

I hung up from my conversation with Sam, and while talking to myself under my breath, I paid the driver. The pen shook in my hand as I wrote a $100 on the second line and signed it. I asked him to fill in the rest. Then, with my stomach rumbling, I moved from the taxi to the police car and held my emotions together. I can't cry. The officer asked me if I wanted anything to drink, I said maybe a coffee. *A hot coffee in this hot Florida weather? I'm not thinking straight, but this is the best I can do right now.* I sipped on the coffee for a bit, trying to calm my nerves. It seemed like this was taking a long time, but I stayed in the car like I was told.

In the police car, I called the funeral home director in Michigan, a woman with whom I had become quite close during Jerry's funeral. She was still in my phone contacts, and was the first person I thought to call. She talked me through what I needed to do. She recommended I demand to go inside the house and see my husband's body. She said I would regret not going in. My children would want to know for sure it was their Dad.

One patient policeman took me inside to view him. "Are you sure you want to do this? I am reluctant to let you see him as his body has started to decay and you might be shocked. The odor is strong. Take your time."

The officer led the way, and I walked closely behind him as we entered the house. I had never seen this home, so my eyes took in the unfamiliar surroundings until we reached the bedroom. Stopping there, right before my eyes, was Ray dressed in his pajamas, lying on the bed in his favorite sleeping position. I placed my hand over my mouth as I stared at his lifeless body. He appeared like he had just quit breathing. I saw a peaceful look on his face, and this was comforting. But, I could only stay a few minutes as it was shocking to see him that way, and the smell was overwhelming. I'll never forget how he looked or that indescribable odor!

They wheeled my husband out of that house on a gurney in a black body bag. I'd told the officer I couldn't bear watching this, and would stand around the side of the house, out of view of their route. But, in the moment, I stole a look anyhow. The sun shone bright in the cloudless sky. Squinting and holding my breath, this didn't seem real. It was like the crime scene in a movie!

I some how got to a Holiday Inn. I don't remember how it happened. On the phone in the hotel room, with tears spilling out of my eyes and running down my cheeks, I talked with a two of my children. Thankfully Sam had already notified my other three daughters and two sons of their dad's sudden passing. I booked a flight for the next day, and then tried to sleep. Ray was now in heaven with his two boys.

On the flight home, I thought, what's ahead now? I was alone. All of the children had moved out of the family home and had gone on with their lives. The big house was familiar, but vacant, and a huge responsibility. I tried not to think of those individual steps I must take to manage life now. I focused on what I had to do tomorrow.

***

Why did I have to include these horrendous scenarios in my memoir? Does anyone reading this need to know? But who could ever predict these things could happen? These and other heartbreaking events of the last sixty years were interspersed with lots of good memories, but I know all had a deep impact on me. Who would ever think one could withstand the pressures of opening the door to find two soldiers informing you of your young son's death? Who would ever think one could remain calm when finding your husband dead when you were supposed to be meeting him for a vacation? When I think about it now, I can't believe those things happened. But they did, and they had a deep impact on my life. Very often, I buried the pain and hid it from others. I've carried on with my life, but deep scars remained below the surface. And I think those remnants have contributed to my behavior with the "man behind the screen."

If I had a friend who'd gone through a similar experience, of trusting a man like Steve Cryer, I would have compassion for her. I would stand by and support her as she recovered. I'm trying to give myself the same consideration, but we're often much harder on ourselves than on our friends.

Ray and I were young and naive. I was eighteen, he was twenty-one when we wed on that memorable July day. Our years together were generally happy, but we hadn't developed our relationship beyond that infatuation stage. We thought it would come naturally. Making babies sure came naturally. Holding back a lot of my feelings, some I didn't even admit to having, resulted in a wedge between us. Early on, we argued a lot, mostly about money and how to spend it, but as the years went by, I just gave in, resulting in fewer confrontations. With seven kids, our lives were busy. We didn't have much time, or didn't make time for ourselves. Date night didn't exist. After I got my education and entered the career world, I was content. We had our own separate lives. In February, 2014, my plan was to make an effort to rekindle our "young love" on that vacation to Florida. Once again, I learned the lesson. I'm not in charge, God is, and even God can't change the past.

Part II

HAPPIER DAYS

During the five years after losing my husband, I was lonely. Being married at eighteen years old, I'd had little experience with dating. Still, I had friends, a large family, attended church every week, and seemed to be busy all the time. A life-long male friend and I had taken a couple of cruises together, and that satisfied the wanderlust in me for a time, but I desired more companionship. So, I joined an online dating site.

I entertained the idea of meeting a gentleman to share a dinner or movie with, or maybe a big bowl of popcorn while cuddling on my couch. I had no intention to remarry. The last forty years taught me marriage takes a lot of work. I don't think I have the energy to do that again!

The first thing you do on a dating website is to create a profile. I was honest about myself on Plenty of Fish. This site has a free section and a paid section. Better pickin's from the paid section, I figured, so I sent the $49.95 payment, which enrolled me for a year, and I was ready to surf the waters. There must be some single man out there looking for a cute old gal like me. I posted a few photos, described myself and an independent and educated woman who is involved in my community.

My profile talked about my career, a retired teacher, and I showed a photo of me leaning against my new sports car. Maybe that would interest some car buffs?

My decision to start dating again might have been a tonic to get through the loneliness, prove I was still desirable, and maybe get a chance at the finer life with a man who could provide it.

4: GROOMING

Spring 2018

....

*"If you can dream and not make dreams
your master... you'll be a man, my son."*

—Rudyard Kipling

....

Soon after posting my profile on PoF, on May 29th, I responded to one gentleman's "Hello." Steve Cryer and I exchanged a few text messages that first day. He was a very nice-looking 61-year-old widower who lived about an hour from me in Ann Arbor, Michigan. His profile stated he was a contractor, and he used sensitive equipment to dig in the ground for whatever the employer needed. He'd also worked in the oil drilling industry. He listed movies and music he liked. I liked the same ones. We enjoyed many of the same books. I was impressed he liked "If" by Rudyard Kipling, one of my favorite poems.

Enamored with his photos, of which he had included several, my imagination started to run wild. I perused his pale blue eyes, strong jawline, spiked gray hair, and thin lips. He appeared to be a slender but muscular guy with nice biceps. I can't stop daydreaming about what's behind that smirk! As he seemed well-educated and experienced in life, I was intrigued. I thought of myself as younger than my chronological age, good health, intelligent, and moderately attractive. *This guy would be getting a fair deal by meeting me! Wonder if he looks as good in person as in the photos?*

One photo of Steve was a selfie of him in his pickup truck, smiling and pointing a finger at the camera. It seemed he had a twinkle in his eyes too. It took little effort to imagine how we could quickly become friends. I sent a similar selfie photo back to him.

From this point on, I'm including the actual messages that were sent as they were written. Also, not all of the messages have been included. I chose these particular ones, as they were details that helped me to connect with him. Early on, I learned about his background. Later, he described his current situation. I've left out those notes that were repeats of earlier ones, and they didn't lend anything more to the story.

April 5, 2018, at 8:30 a.m., Steve Cryer <Stevekevin1000> "Janet, you're a beautiful woman. I like your shiny blue fingernails. I can't wait to meet you. I'll take you to the shop to get them painted. How much does it cost you?"

"Steve, my nails are painted blue to match my sports car. When we meet, I'll drive the Camaro and maybe even let you drive it sometime. Thanks for noticing the nails." I get all tingly inside with this kind of attention.

When I was a young girl, shopping at Goodwill was not uncommon for my mother, three sisters, and me. Mom was a talented sewer and could remodel any dress to appear custom, but we dreamed of someday shopping off the racks of friendly stores like Nordstroms and Saks Fifth Avenue. We learned to be thrifty, sometimes to a fault. Consequently, we often didn't believe we deserved better. Frugality was my mantra as a young wife and mother. We were a one-income family, and I needed to save money somewhere. I sewed a lot, canned vegetables, and shopped at the bulk food store. When I started teaching, I reconsidered some of the old principles. *Maybe I don't need to behave like a "poor" girl anymore?* With my own income, I bought a car that wasn't a van or station wagon and purchased genuine leather boots, a purse, and gloves. I kind of went overboard with my own money.

April 5, 2018, at 8:40 a.m., Steve Cryer <Stevekevin1000> "How long have you been on this website? This is my first time."

"This is my first time too. I sent a short "Hello" to a couple of other guys, but you're the first to get back with me."

Photos on Steve's PoF profile were him at worksites, one at an oil drilling site, wearing a hard hat. *Wow, this guy looks fit, rugged, and undoubtedly fascinating. Maybe he'll be one to share my desire for intrigue and just live it up!*

April 5, 2018, at 8:30 a.m., Steve Cryer <Stevekevin1000> "Janet, I like fast cars too. Someday, I wanna own a Lamborghini. Right now, I have a Dodge Ram pickup, and it's for my job."

I replied: "Steve, driving alone on the open road is relaxing to me. Sometimes it's just the two-hour drive north to my family's cabin. I might stay the night, make a fire and watch old movies, or just have dinner in my favorite restaurant, then drive home the next day. Then I return to real life and daily responsibilities like paying bills and cooking for myself."

April 5, 2018, at 8:45 a.m., Steve Cryer <Stevekevin1000> "Sweetie, that sounds nice. Will you send me a picture of your cabin? Maybe we can go there together some day? I'd like to keep your fire burning and cook a nice dinner for us. Maybe we'd fall asleep together under the blanket watching a movie. Honey, I'm good at most any job and will help at your cabin. Where is it, so I can look for it on a map?"

I replied: "It's on the Rifle River on the eastern side of Michigan." *Damn, I'm not going to give him explicit directions, like an address. Sometimes, I reveal too much, get wrapped up in the conversation, and then let down my defenses. But I do look forward to having a rendezvous with him there.*

April 5, 2018, at 10:00 a.m., Steve Cryer <Stevekevin1000> "I've gotta go to work now, Honey. I'll text you later this afternoon or tonight. Bye."

I wrote: "Sure thing. I should get moving myself, instead of sitting here messaging you all morning. Can we chat later today?"

Steve claimed he'd traveled throughout the states and internationally and was born in Berlin, Germany. *Does he have an accent? Would I even know what a German accent sounded like? I need to get to know his voice, however it sounds.*

Our daily conversations revealed a man who had been lonely for fourteen years after losing his wife. He was financially secure, which was very important to me. I vowed I wouldn't be taken advantage of by someone deep in debt. Ray had left me comfortable, and I could support myself financially but had no intention of taking on a needy partner. *My heart quickened at the thought of dressing up, going to parties, the theatre, concerts, and fine restaurants. What's the harm in getting to know this man?*

April 6, 2018, at 8:20 a.m., Steve Cryer <Stevekevin1000> "Honey, good morning. You are my dream girl, and my parents taught me never to give up on my dreams. I can see us living together and being very happy."

I replied: "First, you said you'd call yesterday afternoon or evening. I was disappointed. Now, let's not get ahead of ourselves, Steve. I need to meet you in person, go on a few dates, and get to know you first! Actually, I've been alone for several years now and I don't think I could tolerate a man friend living with me. I'm very fussy! But, once we've met, I'll invite you over to visit."

April 6, 2018, at 8:45 a.m., Steve Cryer <Stevekevin1000> "Dad was German and Mom was American. She was a good cook, he was handy around the house. We moved to Texas when I was ten. In high school I played basketball and as a tall left-handed forward, I could shoot from either side. I was a high scorer and the girls would chant my name throughout the game. I was embarrassed but liked it."

I wrote: "You make me laugh, Steve. I can imagine you on the basketball court, smiling from ear to ear with all that attention. Did I ever tell you that I am left-handed? It's usually an advantage in sports, but in Kindergarten it's not. We had to learn to cut with those blasted right-handed scissors. I still cut right-handed, even though someone finally invented special ones for those of us in our right mind." Is this guy telling me about his family just to make conversation? Or is there some other reason? I guess, the more I learn about him the better.

April 6, 2018, at 8:50 a.m., Steve Cryer <Stevekevin1000> "Janet, can you swim? Would you swim in the ocean?"

I replied: "I can dog paddle and float so could probably save my life. Absolutely, I would enjoy going to the ocean with you. But the best part would be after swimming, sitting on a blanket beside you and soaking up the sun." *I'm afraid of the ocean, of sharks and stinging things, but I'm not telling him. So, I'll imagine walking barefooted on the beach, and sunbathing with this intriguing man.*

April 6, 2018, at 9:00 a.m., Steve Cryer <Stevekevin1000> "I can teach you. I'm a good swimmer. Honey, where do you live? I own my house, and I love to cook and am a good chef. What's your favorite meal, sweetie?"

I wrote: "Wow, you have a lot of questions. Let me see: I like Italian, Mexican and good old American food. But I do like someone to wait on me and treat me like a princess. Maybe we can prepare dinner together sometime. My husband and I built our home forty years ago. It has four bedrooms for my large family. I had a big vegetable garden every summer, and we raised chickens for a couple of years. I could have been a pioneer woman, I think. Anyhow, we made lots of memories!"

April 6, 2018, at 9:20 a.m., Steve Cryer <Stevekevin1000> "Have you traveled much? I worked in several states including Texas, and in China and South America. I had one contract in Great Britain where my partner and I lost a lot of money. We dug for several weeks and didn't find anything. Would you lose respect for me if you knew how much money I lost and I failed?"

I replied: "No, Steve, it's part of the business. You win some and lose some. I'm happy to report that I've taken several river cruises through Europe and love the little towns, in answer to your question." *Maybe if he knows I've traveled, he won't try to stretch his own stories? He sure seems boastful about himself. Is he telling me his own life story to get additional information out of me? I need to be cautious about what I share until I get to know him better. This guy is moving fast.*

April 6, 2018, at 9:45 a.m., Steve Cryer <Stevekevin1000> "I've earned two Master's degrees, in Engineering and Geology, and own two homes, one in Michigan and one in Texas. Dad and I built the house in Texas together and it's beautiful and huge. I want to give you the code to the alarm system at my houses."

I wrote: "Steve, why would you give me the code. I don't even know where your houses are? You sent me a photo of your house in Ann Arbor, but it could be any house. If you give me the address I'll drive by someday. *But, wow, two Master's Degrees? You must have started those programs right out of high school?*" *I'll look up the San Antonio College he talked about attending and see what degrees they offer. I need to check this out. Maybe he's using the word "masters degree" to mean something other than the level of study?*

April 6, 2018, at 9:55 a.m., Steve Cryer <Stevekevin1000> "Janet, I want you to know I trust you. Memorize the code. Don't write it down and put it in your purse. I use this code for everything I own. I told you I've earned a lot of money, and I want my hard-earned money to be safe."

"Trust goes both ways, Steve. Keep that in mind." *He's embellishing his story. But I get excited to talk with him, and I'm not going to let go of this opportunity. Dear Lord, I'm thankful for the last 60 years of my life, for my devoted family and loyal friends. I'm taking this dating journey cautiously, but I'm pleading for the wisdom to make sound decisions as I go forward. I'm comforted you hear my prayers and will walk beside me each day. I'll give nephew, John a call. As a seasoned detective, maybe he can give me some advice.*

"Hi, Aunt Janet. What's going on with you lately?"

"John, I've subscribed to an online dating site and have been talking to a man who lives in Ann Arbor. I'm thinking of meeting him in person. What do you think about it? You're experienced in these matters, and you're my nephew, so I figured you'd give me good advice.

"Aunt Janet, I'd say meet him during the daytime, at a public place, and tell someone you trust about your plan. You're the most intelligent woman I know. You have a Ph.D. in common sense, so be careful, and you'll be fine.

April 6, 2018, at 3:45 p.m., Steve Cryer <Stevekevin1000> "I enjoyed texting with you this morning. You're easy to talk to. I wanted to tell you about my daughter, Selina. She's thirteen, almost fourteen. After my wife passed, her grandparents helped me out. They live in Missouri and care for her while I'm away at work. I just came back from a vacation with her. We went to California and swam in the ocean. I'd like to bring her to Michigan to live with me. Do you think I could? Would you help me get her enrolled in school? You were a teacher and I trust your experience and wisdom. I am happy I found you. You're just what I needed."

I responded: "Yes, I think you could bring Selina to live with you. Lots of single dads care for their daughters. Would you enroll her in public or private school? I know the Ann Arbor schools are well respected. I can help you get her enrolled, to choose her classes and go shopping for clothes and school supplies." So I'm just what he needed?

He'd better not be looking for a mother for his daughter. This had better be about he and I.

April 6, 2018, at 4:00 p.m., Steve Cryer <Stevekevin1000> "Oh, Janet. I'd put her in private school for sure. I can afford it, and I want her to be safe."

Steve doesn't seem to know anything about the public school system in Ann Arbor. So, why is he more concerned about his daughter's safety than the academics a school could provide? Is he thinking of the Columbine tragedy? Does he think people with large bank accounts are vulnerable, and their kids need extra security? It seems to be an overly protective attitude.

April 7, 2018, at 4:30 p.m., Steve Cryer <Stevekevin1000> "Honey, what are you having for dinner tonight? I'm making chicken pot pies, from a recipe my mother gave me. I'll send you a photo of them. Hold on a few minutes while I take out all this trash."

I wrote: "HOLY COW! You can really cook, and you clean up after yourself? The photo of two pies in the oven looks like you'll have left overs for tomorrow. I hope the meal is as tasty as it looks. By the way, I meant to ask you earlier, why did you have a California area code on your phone number?"

April 7, 2018, at 4:45 p.m., Steve Cryer <Stevekevin1000> "I knew you would ask me this. On the vacation last month with Selina I dropped and broke my phone, so I had to get a new one. This one is an iPhone X and has a local area code. Damn this phone takes good pictures. I'll send you one."

I wrote: "I'm not complaining, but how are you able to spend so much time texting me? You could've transferred your number to the new phone, you know. But, I enjoy the companionship. It's almost like you're here with me and we're having a lovely conversation. I enjoy the photos you've been sending. Keep it up! I spend way too much time staring at your photos, you handsome man! I hope I'm not preventing you from doing your work."

April 7, 2018, at 4:55 p.m., Steve Cryer <Stevekevin1000> "No, Honey, some days I work long hours, but then other days I can take time off. I bid on projects and work until they're finished. I don't work by the hour, but hope I'm able to retire soon. And I enjoy texting with you, and it never gets boring. You're a sweet woman."

I was proud of myself for doing the research, like checking the area code on his phone. He keeps up with the newest technology, like the iPhone X. I expect that with the business he's in. A few details did seem sketchy, the Master's degrees, his daughter living with grandparents, and his general boasting. This long-distance relationship, behind the screen, allowed both of us to reveal selected bits of our story. I suspect we both were doing so quite frequently.

April 7, 2018, at 6:30 p.m., Steve Cryer <Stevekevin1000> "How long were you married Janet, and how long have you been widowed?" *I'm reluctant to discuss these personal details with this man I don't know, but I'll give him a brief overview to answer his questions.*

I wrote: "I was married for forty-four years, and five years ago Ray was suddenly taken from me when he died in his sleep. We had a good marriage, but I was so busy running a household with seven kids that we didn't have much time for ourselves. Now, the evenings alone are difficult. Even after an exhausting day it's not easy to get to sleep. I keep busy during the day. And I have a deep faith in God." *I know Steve's set up this questioning so he can come back with his own story.*

April 7, 2018, at 7:10 p.m., Steve Cryer <Stevekevin1000> "I'm sorry to hear of your loss, Janet. You're too young to live the rest of your life alone. Helena and I were married almost ten years. I lost her fourteen years ago. I was in the Army and stationed in Afghanistan when she was pregnant with our first child. I had a three-day leave, but couldn't leave the country, so she was coming to me. She hated when I was gone from her. I didn't want her to fly in her condition, but she had a strong mind. The plane crashed on the way and she died, but our baby girl lived. After that I retired from the Army and came back to Missouri to help my in-laws raise the baby. Selina is thirteen now and will enter high school in the fall."

Jerry was in the Army a short time, but I don't think the military gives three-day leaves to soldiers while on deployment in Afghanistan. I'm skeptical of a woman being allowed on a plane when she was eight months into her pregnancy, indeed big and fat, showing a lot. How could she get a flight to Afghanistan anyhow? I need to do some research about the plane crash. Quickly doing the math in my head, his age would be about thirty-five when he got married, forty-six when he had his first child. He was a sixty-year-old guy raising a fourteen-year-old girl. What a challenge for anyone!

I wrote: "I'm sorry to hear about your loss. Losing a spouse is tragic at any age. But I can see how you're so protective of your only child. I too, know grief and loss. I look forward to telling you about my son, Jerry who was killed in action in Afghanistan. We'll have much to share. I think of you so often Steve and dream of some happiness for the both of us. I'm glad you suggested we end the day with a prayer. I'll say the prayer tonight, and you can take the next night. 'Dear Lord, thank you for this day, for my friends and family, and for this growing relationship with Steve. May we learn to appreciate and support each other as the days go by. Amen.'"

April 7, 2018, at 9:10 p.m., Steve Cryer <Stevekevin1000> "Sweet dreams, my Queen."

5: MEETING UP

Mid-June 2018

....

"You're only human. You live once and life is wonderful, so eat the damned red velvet cupcake."

—Emma Stone

....

Steve and I had been corresponding for many weeks. I was eager to see him. He went along with my proposal to meet somewhere, to get to know each other in a face-to-face setting. We texted almost every day but hadn't yet talked on the phone, so we hadn't heard each other's voices. He put me off, and said we'd talk soon. I was on edge, not at all confident in his reaction to seeing me in person. Women dwell on their physical appearance way too much!

Some friends of mine invited me to a local coffee shop that offered live music on some nights. It was a quaint place where I had attended other events, so I shared this idea with my new friend Steve, asked him if he wanted to go with me, and he agreed. *Being with my friends might give me a comfortable environment to meet this mystery man. We won't be alone, so I'll feel safe. Also, the background music will help ease the tensions of the first meeting. Steve listed in his PoF profile several dozen musical groups he liked, so maybe he'll enjoy this musical event.*

June 11, 2018, at 11:10 p.m., Steve Cryer <Stevekevin1000> "How are you doing sweetie? How was your night?"

I replied: "It was horrible! Are you kidding? You were supposed to call me tonight on your way to my house. We talked about it extensively yesterday." I was texting rapidly, not waiting for a reply. "I want you to know I waited until the last minute, then gave up on you and drove myself to the concert. You agreed to go with me, and to pick me up at my house. It's now 11:00. I should be in bed sleeping, but I'm so mad I can't even think about shutting my eyes. My friends advised me to immediately cut off all communication with you, and they helped me to block your number. They realized I was upset. But, after I got back home home, I relented and unblocked you because I had to let you know how disappointed I was. You stood me up! Can you imagine how embarrassed I was in front of my friends when I tried to explain why I was there as a party of one? It's pathetic!"

June 11, 2018, at 11:12 p.m., Steve Cryer <Stevekevin1000> "You mean you weren't gonna talk to me ever again?"

I replied: "Yes, that's exactly what I mean."

June 11, 2018, at 11:15 p.m., Steve Cryer <Stevekevin1000> "I had to stay late at work tonight, and I told you before, sometimes this happened. I even told you sometimes I stayed at the job site and slept a little while, then went back to work. I tried to call you a few minutes ago, but you didn't answer."

I was still livid. My eyes were stinging from holding back a cry. I wrote: "I didn't receive any phone call from you tonight! You're lying! You couldn't even text me, that this might happen tonight, that you might not be able to join me? It would be a thoughtful thing to do. I blocked your number. Don't you get it? I am crushed and disappointed to be disrespected this way."

June 11, 2018, at 11:20 p.m., Steve Cryer <Stevekevin1000> "Well, I guess I probably shouldn't have agreed to come with you at all. I pretty much knew I wouldn't be able to attend."

I wrote: "So, actually you lied to me."

June 11, 2018, at 11:30 p.m., Steve Cryer <Stevekevin1000> "I'm sorry. Please, Baby, don't ever block my number again. I love you and want to be with you. I can't bear thinking you wouldn't talk to me again. I told you I haven't talked to another woman, like we are, since my wife died fourteen years ago. I love texting with you every morning, and every evening before we go to sleep. I'll do the prayer tonight. 'Thank you, Lord, for bringing Janet into my life. Protect her this night, and help me to make her happy. Amen.'"

Weak under his spell and possibly falling in love with him, I excused this last mishap. I was still so full of hope. *I guess this is just a little misunderstanding, and I shouldn't make a big deal about it. But now my friends know I'm talking with a guy online. They must think I'm pretty naive.* After this incident, I was more cautious and hid information from friends and family because I wanted to avoid any possible embarrassment?

I wrote: "Steve, here's a photo of me in my bathroom mirror. I just curled my hair. I don't have any makeup on yet, but do you like what you see?"

June 25, 2018, at 11:30 a.m., Steve Cryer <Stevekevin1000> "Janet, you look so cute. I can stand behind you, and kiss your neck. When I come home I can help you brush your hair too. You will like it."

For the next couple of weeks, Steve and I amicably corresponded. I got past the disappointment because I craved the "relationship" we seemed to be developing, albeit frustrating at times. And I hadn't seen or talked with him face-to-face yet. I longed to share intimate moments with my partner, to sit out on my patio in the evening with a glass of wine, and enjoy the night sky together. I wanted this relationship to be real! Steve had revealed a bit of his imperfect character, but no one is perfect, including me. Still, I had plans in mind to ease my doubts regarding his integrity.

I resolved that if he were going to avoid coming to me, I'd go to him. I'd make it so effortless and make him an offer he couldn't refuse. I'd get a hotel room for myself in Ann Arbor and invite him for a visit. Who'd turn down an offer to meet the woman he'd declared he wanted to be with? I had no fears of driving the distance or staying in a hotel by myself. I'd conquered that problem long ago. My friends and I had stayed at this Webster Inn in Ann Arbor the previous summer, so it was familiar to me and my first choice for the rendezvous. The excitement level increased by the minute as I planned this event, selecting the perfect clothes, jewelry, and perfume. At the corner gas station, I filled the tank in the Camaro and drove it through the car wash. Then, with my bags packed and my fearless attitude, I prepared to take the chariot to the task.

Keeping the details to myself, I did mention to my daughter, Marie, and my friend, Mary Ann, that I was going out of town for a couple of days of rest and relaxation. They accepted my explanation that reading, swimming in the pool, and shopping would help me. I could shop the farmer's markets for essential items to help the body relax, including the bar soap and lotions I had gotten there during my previous visit. I had a fluffy historical novel to read, one of those paperbacks you find at the grocery store check-out. Hoping there wouldn't be too many visitors in the middle of the week, the hotel pool might even be empty. And that would be nice.

On July 3, I shared my plans with Steve.

July 3, 2018, at 11:45 a.m., Steve Cryer <Stevekevin1000> "Ya, Baby it would be nice to have you nearby. We could enjoy a dinner together and relax and talk. I don't know where that hotel is, but I can find it. My heart calls out to you. Honey, I may have to take my truck into the shop today. I heard a funny noise coming from the front end. I'll get it looked at right away. I don't want to break down somewhere. I'll text you later this afternoon about it."

I responded, "I'm thrilled to finally be able to see and talk to you, my dear man. This is like the secret rendezvous I've been dreaming about for weeks. I made the reservations, started doing my laundry and am packing my bags. I can't wait to see you. Hope your truck repair turns out to be something simple."

July 3, 2018, at 4:15 p.m., Steve Cryer <Stevekevin1000> "Janet, I wanted to let you know I have a late meeting tonight. I'll text you when I'm driving home."

My reply was: "No problem, dear. I'll be busy preparing for the drive to your neck of the woods and choosing an attractive outfit for our first meeting." Humming to myself as I went about the duties of leaving my house for a couple of days, my mind was racing. My skin was warm to the touch, so I stood under the ceiling fan for a few minutes. *That feels better!* I squinted in the magnified mirror on my bathroom counter, counting the facial wrinkles. I did a complete facial to reduce the wrinkles before leaving home. I was hungry, which reminded me I needed to prepare to wait for a little while at the hotel, so I gathered some granola bars, cheese, crackers, and red apples, which are aphrodisiacs.

July 3, 2018, at 10:05 p.m., Steve Cryer <Stevekevin1000> "I'm not happy, Honey. I don't know how to tell you this, but I need to leave the country and be gone for up to a month. I've accepted this last contract in Dubai before I retire. It's a great opportunity. I can't turn it down."

I texted, "That's not such bad news. At least we'll be able to see each other at the hotel before you go." I was daydreaming about checking into the Webster, getting comfortable, and texting him that I was there.

37

July 3, 2018, at 10:15 p.m., Steve Cryer <Stevekevin1000> "No, Honey, I need to leave tomorrow morning at 4:00 a.m. for the long flight to Dubai, UAE. But the good thing is, I'll just be gone a month or maybe two."

Quickly typing, I wrote: "What? You didn't know or even suspect this before the meeting? I'm confused and disappointed. Why didn't you give me a heads up that you might have a job offer? So, now I'm sure you didn't plan on seeing me in person at all!"

I prayed daily for the grace to accept God's will. Most recently, my prayer was how and if I should carry on the distant relationship with Steve Cryer. As I sat in church the Sunday after learning of Steve's upcoming job, I prayed for a sign. Was I supposed to continue talking to him or not? The word *Dubai* came to mind. I interpreted this thought as a fair warning to stay away from him. Who goes to Dubai anyhow? Big rollers, CEOs of Fortune 500 companies. This guy Steve wasn't any of those. I thought it might just be a test to see if I would hang on, allow him into my life and wait for him to come home to Michigan.

I sent a message: "I'm sorry, but I won't accept any more emails or texts from you. I plan to go back to POF and restart my account. I'm not waiting a month or two." I hope I never hear from him again! That will make it easier to let him go.

6: EARNING MY TRUST

Early July 2018

....

"If you can keep your head while all about you are losing theirs and blaming it on you... You'll be a man, my son."

—Rudyard Kipling

....

I was done with Steve. Swore off the fool! I prayed for direction. God's answer: You're not in charge. I am.

July 15, 2018, at 11:00 a.m., Steve Cryer <Stevekevin1000> "Faith, believe and trust is all i need from u at this point of time."

I sat like a statue in my kitchen chair as I stared at those words. This was the first I'd heard from Steve since my declaration to move on a month ago. Should I respond? It would prove to both of us I couldn't keep promises.

Timidly, I wrote: "I told you I'm not interested in waiting for you, and I'd go back to Plenty of Fish. I never even met you face-to-face. There've been other men interested in getting to know me, and I've been writing back and forth with them. There are other fish in the sea!" *I know by responding at all, I am reopening the line of communication, but I can't control myself. No other PoF guy has shown any interest. They say we live too far apart, or*

I'm not the petite athletic woman they want to date. Steve asks about Mom, the kids and grandkids, the cats, and how I'm feeling. I told him I wouldn't accept his emails or texts, but I didn't block him and watched every day for his message. What am I doing? He isn't ready to give up, and I'm not either.

July 15, 2018, at 11:20 a.m., Steve Cryer <Stevekevin1000> "Honey, I hope I'll be able to come home in three or four weeks. That's not so long. After this job I'll retire and we'll be able to spend time together. Please be patient."

I replied: "I'm not so sure I want to wait. I'll think about it and let you know." I received a short and sweet email every morning and evening from then on. *How can he miss me like he says? He's never even met me? But I miss him, at least I miss his typed messages! Dear Lord, please let me know this is real.*

Steve was beginning to share more, like how he felt about living in a foreign city all alone. I was encouraged, energized, and content for the time being. Unfortunately, we couldn't talk on the phone as he claimed Verizon had a poor connection where he was and that his plan didn't include international calls. *Why didn't he arrange to add that feature to his account before he left Michigan? I would've done that first, once knowing about the trip, mainly to communicate with me, the sweet woman he missed so much.*

July 15, 2018, at 11:50 a.m., Steve Cryer <Stevekevin1000> "Hey Love, please work on the hangouts app. OK? This texting sucks! I really miss you...Xoxo"

I finally successfully added the app to my phone but overlooked a lot of grammar, punctuation, and spelling errors in his messages. I rationalized he was probably typing fast or using dictation mode. Maybe his accent was difficult for the app to spell his words correctly. The messages through Hangouts were shorter than those he'd texted.

July 16, 2018, at 4:00 p.m., Steve Cryer <Hangouts> "Honey, I'm sending you a video of myself here in Dubai, cause I know you miss me. Tell me what you think?"

Opening the attachment, I stared at a grainy video of a man lying in bed. His lips were moving, and I strained to hear what he was saying. It sounded like, "Honey, I've just finished my days work and am resting now. Give me a little cuddles." The man held out his arms for a hug. And even though the sound quality on the video wasn't very clear, his voice sounded like an Irish brogue. The voice and the facial movements didn't sync up, like it was dubbed over another video. I played it over several times to try to figure it out. *I hope to hell this is not Steve cause this man gives me the creeps. He does resemble the man in the photos, but there's something that seems off.*

I wrote: "Steve, I'm not convinced that's you in the video, and it kinda makes me sick to my stomach seeing that creepy looking guy lying on his bed trying to give someone, me, a kiss. What made you think I'd like to see that?"

July 16, 2018, at 4:20 p.m., Steve Cryer <Hangouts> "Sweetie, my friends told me to send it to you, and that if you saw it, you might be convinced I was real. I guess it wasn't a good idea. No, it's not really me, and I'm sorry you didn't like it. But, we're meant to be together. Just be patient, please. Honey, after a long day at work, I sit in the restaurant doing calculations on the computer. Maybe you'll like this picture better. I'm sitting at the bar with my computer."

He admits the video is not him. Thank the Lord! This guy is disgusting. His friends are disgusting too, to think I'd be impressed when I saw it. Maybe he's worried I'll give up on him, which would be so easy to do for some women. I'm committed to seeing him first before I do that. But, this Dubai job won't be finished in a couple of weeks, and I know it.

The photo he sent showed the same person I'd gotten to know from his other photos, sitting at a bar, looking at his laptop computer, not at all like the guy in the video on the bed. Thank the Lord! A light brown colored drink in a tall glass stood next to the laptop. I was pleased he tried to keep me apprised of his daily routine.

I asked: "Are you drinking a beer? I'm sure it's pretty hot there in Dubai. You're wearing a sweatshirt, so maybe it's not that warm after all?" I stared at these photos for hours, trying to imagine him at work in Dubai.

July 16, 2018, at 6:00 p.m., Steve Cryer <Hangouts> "Honey, you know I don't drink beer. That's apple juice in the glass."

I replied: "Oh, really? I guarantee it would be much stronger if it was mine, but way back in April you did say you didn't go to bars or drink anything alcoholic. But I still remember you said there was a sixteen-year-old, unopened bottle of scotch on the shelf in your house in Ann Arbor, and that you'd serve me a glass when you got back to town."

July 16, 2018, at 9:00 p.m., Steve Cryer <Hangouts> "Janet, dear, I'd be happy to crack open that bottle of scotch for you. Your'e a beautiful person, inside and out. After I get back home I want to take us on a trip to Dubai. It's a beautiful city. We can have a nice dinner in the restaurant at the top of the tallest building in the city. I'm gonna enjoy seeing you dressed up in a fancy gown. Good night, Honey."

July 17, 2018, at 11:00 a.m., Steve Cryer <Hangouts> "Selina's fourteenth birthday is coming up, and I won't be there again. I promised her this year would be different. Janet, what do you think I should send Selina for her birthday?"

I said: "I suggest a bracelet or necklace. Girls always like jewelry. You'd certainly be able to find something lovely in Dubai." I had five granddaughters, ages six to eighteen, and was experienced in this area. I knew what they liked and didn't like. Money was always a sure bet. He ignored my suggestion and flatly declared:

July 17, 2018, at 11:10 a.m., Steve Cryer <Hangouts> "She wants a laptop computer. Her piano teacher said if she had one, she'd install music software so she can practice her lessons."

My generous heart pumped in my chest as I imagined this fourteen-year-old girl without her father for her birthday. But, on the other hand, maybe she was serious about learning to play the piano, and I could help.

I wrote: "I can purchase a laptop for you at Best Buy and mail it to her."

July 17, 2018, at 11:20 a.m., Steve Cryer <Hangouts> "Honey, it's so kind of you to offer to help me out. Keep the receipt, and I'll pay you back when I get home. She only needs a basic model.

Wouldn't he attempt to get the most expensive computer out of me, especially after I quickly volunteered to do so? I was convinced he's not conning me, but that he's a genuine guy and a thoughtful dad.

Steve's instructions were to mail the package through the Post Office to: Seth Asamoah Jnr, in Springfield Gardens, New York.

The next day I purchased a Lenovo laptop for $379.99 ($402 with tax) and mailed it to the address he gave me. I also bought a pretty case for it, spending an additional $39, and wrote on the card that the case was from me, 'Daddy's friend.' Nervous was an understatement as I stood in line at the post office, and dubious the clerk might question the weird address or the spelling of Junior. This might be my last opportunity to reconsider sending a gift to someone I've never met. But I so desperately want to please this man and for it to be real, so he will come back home and want to be with me. I am anxious that Steve would realize I am the one for him. Am I ready for this?

When the line moved forward, and it was my turn, I was forced to face the postal employee but avoided giving him direct eye contact. He read the address label on the neat package I'd prepared, entered the information into his computer, and promptly printed out a label. I paid the $12.50 postage and $6.80 for insurance with my debit card. He didn't seem to have any questions at all, so I breathed a sigh of relief. He handed me the receipt with the tracking number. I whispered, "Thank you," and discreetly walked out of the office. Once in my car, breathing normally again, I took a photo of the receipt with my iPhone and immediately sent it off to Steve.

I texted, "Steve, you should have the receipt now, but who lives in New York? You said Selina lives with her grandparents in Missouri. I don't care, but is her grandfather African? Asamoah is an African name. And he is a Junior? Is Jnr a typo?"

July 17, 2018, at 11:40 a.m., Steve Cryer <Stevekevin1000> "Yes, Seth is her grandfather, and no, he's not a black man. That address is a mailbox where people who don't have permanent addresses can receive mail."

After he'd given me this unusual address, I researched online and found it was for Aramak International Courier. The description said many international contractors would use these "mailboxes" to send and receive their mail when they were away from home. The company sent mail and packages to Asia, Africa, and Europe. Still curious after reading this, I wondered why he would need to use that mail system. I was mailing the computer to Selina in Missouri.

I replied: "But didn't you say Selina lived in Missouri with her grandparents, and New York is probably1000 miles away?"

July 17, 2018, at 11:50 a.m., Steve Cryer <Hangouts> "No, sweetie, you must've misunderstood. Seth is her grandpa, and he'll pick it up and give it to her."

I knew I wasn't wrong about where he told me his daughter lived, but I decided to let it go for now. I gathered quite a lot of questions to ask, as soon as I had the chance. Better start a list, so I don't forget! He would certainly be appreciative of my little favor to make his daughter's birthday special.

Four days later, I received the first email from Selina,

July 21, 2018, at 3:50 p.m., Selina Cryer <Selina30K> "Mummy, thank you for the birthday gift. I'm happy to have the computer. Now my piano teacher will install software to help me practice at home. I still miss Daddy, though."

Why didn't she mention the case I included in the box? I'm surprised she still calls Steve Daddy and addresses me as Mummy. Maybe Daddy is just a term of endearment she's used as a child and hasn't abandoned it just because she's now a teenager. But, Mummy? I'm going to have to clarify with Steve. I'm never going to be his daughter's mother, and she shouldn't address me as such.

***

The third week of July in Michigan, the trees and flowers were in full bloom. I'd taken a couple of days to get away from home and the responsibilities of taking care of a house, staying at the Best Western Hotel in St. Ignace. I'd stayed there before with friends, so this was a comfortable relaxation spot. Walking the beach of Lake Superior in the Upper Peninsula, I picked up five or six colored stones, or maybe it was beach glass, took a picture of them in my hand, and sent it to Steve. I missed his attention and wished he could be with me on this serene beach.

July 22, 2018, at 11:45 a.m., Steve Cryer <Hangouts> "It looks like you've found quartz, basalt, agates and a piece of glass."

Did he know his geology, or were these just remnants of a Pepsi bottle, Mountain Dew, and some weathered beach stones? I was surprised he would respond so quickly with any answer at all. But now, after getting a reply from him, I was once again encouraged by his interest in me and was ready to return to Michigan's lower peninsula and proceed with the plans for getting Steve home. Checking out of the hotel early that next morning, I jumped into my Camaro and put the pedal to the metal. The four-hour drive gave me time to do a lot of thinking. Once at home, I noticed a new text message from Steve.

July 22, 2018, at 4:00 p.m., Steve Cryer <Hangouts> "Honey, I have a big problem."

7: OVERWHELMED

Last week of July 2018

....

Murphy's Law—If anything can go wrong, it will.

....

July 23, 2018, at 1:00 p.m., Steve Cryer <Hangouts> "Honey, I have a big problem. I left my wallet in a Uber car here in Dubai. I had all of my identification and money in it. I made many phone calls to get the wallet back, but I couldn't. I'm so frustrated."

I replied: "I suggest you go to the US Embassy office in Dubai for help. People tell me a person can get temporary identification in a day or two. Lost wallets or purses happen all the time while abroad. Did you carry all your money with you? Don't you have credit or debit cards? They can be reissued in a day or so."

July 23, 2018, at 1:20 p.m., Steve Cryer <Hangouts> "Janet, I don't use charge cards, just cash, and to be safe I keep everything in my wallet. This is a foreign country and there are thieves all over. Before I can leave, I need to pay rental fees on the equipment I used, pay the hotel bill, and buy a plane ticket. Can you lend me $5000? I'll pay you back as soon as I get home. I have three million US dollars in Bank of America. I can afford this."

I answered: "You're a big boy. Figure it out! Don't you have any friends? I can't lend you any money. I'm a widow and need to take care of myself. I can't rely on other people. So I need to keep my money."

I walked around my house, shaking my head repeatedly, staring at my phone in anticipation of another pleading message from Steve, and shuffling from room to room. Would he retrieve his wallet somehow, or someone other than me would save his butt? Sitting in my reading chair, I rocked back and forth, attempting to come to grips with Steve's request. Was it a reasonable one? No, for sure, it was not. Still, maybe I could figure out a way to help him.

It was crushing not to hear from him for the balance of the day, and I was almost certain this was our breaking point. Weeping quietly, I asked myself, "Would he give up on me if I didn't *Stand By Your Man*, as the country star Tammy Wynette sings? Did he care enough for me to respect my financial needs and keep in touch even though I wouldn't lend him the funds?

The following day, I messaged him, "How're you doing, Steve? Solve your problem yet?"

July 24, 2018, at 9:58 a.m., Steve Cryer <Hangouts> "No, and now I have another problem because you wouldn't help me out right away. The company was ready to pay me for the job, but I hadn't returned and paid for the equipment rental after losing my wallet. So, now the manager is out of town, and he was the only one who could write me a check. But the foreman could pay me in gold bars. So I accepted them, 200 of them. They each weigh one kilogram (2.205 pounds) for a total of eleven million dollars. I brought them back to the hotel. The bars are under my bed now and I'm afraid to go out of my room for fear of being robbed."

I replied, "You're on your own." *Gold bars? Eleven million dollars? Preposterous!*

July 24, 2018, at 10:15 a.m., Steve Cryer <Hangouts> "That's what I expected you to say, but Honey, I still consider us soul mates, and please find a place in your heart to make this work. I have faith in you and believe in you. I'll repay every penny you send. Calm down and think about it for awhile."

I wanted to help him get home and had already come to his aid with his daughter's birthday gift. I wouldn't be borrowing any money and had $5000 in my checking account, which I could temporarily lend him until next month's bills came due. He promised he'd repay me as soon as he got home, which, if everything worked out, could be in a week or so. For direction, I turned to my Bible and the Beatitudes, especially the part that says, "Blessed are you who are poor, for the kingdom of God is yours. *I'm not going to worry about being poor, and I won't ever be, but I'm not sure about lending this large amount of money.*

July 24, 2018, at 4:18 p.m., Steve Cryer <Hangouts> "Honey, I feel so lonely in this foreign city. Everything is out of my control. I haven't even been eating, just hanging out in this room. I beg you to help me somehow."

I imagined him confined to his bed, fearful of losing the payment for his month of hard work. He seemed overwhelmed! He hadn't pushed me or made me feel guilty for not agreeing to lend money, but instead, he sent me sweet messages and YouTube songs almost every day.

My heart and resolve were softened when he sent a particularly touching song. I imagined Steve and I slow dancing to the gentle melody. I could almost feel his breath as he sang the lyrics to me that promise that he would always stand by me through good times and bad. Believing that he meant those words, I began to believe that my devotion to him should be just as strong.

My hands shook as I touched the keypad of my phone, "I'll lend you the $5000. But I'll need it returned to me in a week to pay my utility and charge card bills."

July 24, 2018, at 6:10 p.m., Steve Cryer <Hangouts> "Janet, you make me very happy. Thank you for trusting me. Did you get the song I sent you, and I mean every word? I'm working so hard to come to you. You complete me! By the way, did you know the Arabs have designed a powerful car, the Devel Sixteen. It can reach a top speed of 348 mph. Look it up on the internet. It's beautiful. But, right now I'm working to get all the documents to ship the gold to the United States. But I need a destination with an address in the states. Would you allow me to use your name and address on the boxes? Could I have them delivered to your house?"

I said: "NO! That's a lot to ask. If you're afraid of being robbed, then how about me? I'd be nervous about having the gold at my house. I don't think it's a smart thing for me to do." *I don't think shipping the boxes to me is a good idea, but I'm already into it, so I'll see if I can steer him away from this plan.*

July 24, 2018, at 6:15 p.m., Steve Cryer <Hangouts> "OK, Honey, I don't want to put you in danger. How about I use my name and your address on the labels? I'll be home in Michigan in a few days and will come to your house to get the gold. Then we can go to my bank, deposit it and I'll pay you back the money you gave me. I already owe you so much. I'm sending you a song to tell you how I feel. Steve sent me a link to the very romantic Hello by Lionel Richie. I listened to the song repeatedly, thinking of him kissing me as it played.

I replied to his message: "Okay, Steve, you can use my address with your name. I don't know why I do these favors for you. Mostly because I want you back in Michigan, for us to meet in person. I'm eager to see your handsome face."

Photos of two large shiny silver boxes labeled in colossal block lettering came across my phone. The first line was Steve Kevin Cryer with my address below. A picture says a thousand words! I imagined the UPS delivery truck driving up my driveway, the man putting those two boxes on a cart and wheeling them up to my porch. *I hope I can get them inside the house by myself.* What if the neighbors saw and wanted to know what was going on? What if my kids or friends were visiting at that time? I'd have a lot of explaining to do!

Then, another text arrived with a photo attached. The picture showed a silver metal box about the size of my most oversized suitcase, opened to reveal twenty or so shiny gold bars, each about the size of a pound box of butter. Damn, if that didn't look real to me!

I wrote: "So, Steve how do I get the $5000 to you?"

July 24, 2018, at 9:10 p.m., Steve Cryer <Hangouts> "I have a friend in Washington, Seth Asamoah Jnr, and he will help me. He has a Chase Bank account. Do you have a Chase Account, and would you be able to transfer money from your account to his? You're so sweet to agree to this, Janet. I'll show my gratitude when we get together back in Michigan."

Isn't this the same person I mailed Selina's computer to? In New York? I'll certainly ask about this bit of information. Very soon too!

I responded, "I'll do some calling and ask about transferring funds. I've never done it before and am mighty nervous. I wouldn't do this for just anyone, you know."

It was the morning of July 25th at 9:00 a.m. I cautiously ventured into a Chase bank nearby. I didn't want to do this in my town. I didn't want to take a chance anyone would recognize me. It was my private business. Even idle chatting with an acquaintance would make me nervous. I was nervous enough about this new experience. It was a big deal transferring any money at all, but most especially to someone I didn't know. I'd be so embarrassed if the bank wouldn't allow the transaction for some reason. I wondered, could Steve and his friend Seth access my account and get more of my money? If anything bad happens, I'll run straight out the front door, jump in my car, and sob. I'm a big chicken sometimes.

To my surprise, the young bank manager was friendly and helpful. I acted naive and uncomfortable with handling this transaction by myself online and told him I'd come to ask for his assistance. He was so willing to walk me through the process. I couldn't have done it without his direction.

The manager said: "Will you be transferring money to Seth's account again sometime?"

I replied: "I hope not sir, as this is a lot of money." I was apprehensive about answering his questions, which, surprisingly, did not include anything about how I knew Seth. I wanted to help my new friend get home, so I rationalized that Steve only needed this help now, and afterward, he was on his own. I was growing very fond of the man. I cared about his welfare wanted to help him return to his life in Michigan with his daughter. *I prayed: Compassionate Father, help me use my resources for the good of the poor.*

July 25th, at 10:00 a.m., I sent a message: "Babe, I was uneasy at the bank. I made it through it all, but hope I never will need to repeat this experience. Truly, I'm anxious for the day we can meet and get to know each other." *Can I even wish for a life-long partner, and can Steve fill that bill? I mustn't forget to ask him who Seth Jnr is.*

July 25, 2018, at 1:10 p.m., Steve Cryer <Hangouts> "Seth called me to say he received the money you transferred. It'll take three days before he's able to transfer it out, where I can withdraw here in Dubai. I'm proud of you my beautiful Queen. With you in my life, my life is complete. We fit together like puzzle pieces. I love you. There are UNICEF offices worldwide, so Seth deposited your money into an account in Washington and I can withdraw it in Dubai. I'll use it to pay the expenses I told you about, and then come back home."

Steve sent me a photo of his plane ticket. It showed he would fly from Dubai to Ghana, Africa to London to Chicago to Detroit. It had his name printed on the ticket: Steve kevin Cryer. It seemed legitimate, but I thought the lower case letter in his middle name must be a typo.

I asked: "Why didn't you fly to Amsterdam? I've flown direct flights from Detroit to Amsterdam and back. This would save going through all those airports with your large package."

July 25, 2018, at 3:10 p.m., Steve Cryer <Hangouts> "This way is cheaper, especially purchasing it only two days before departure. I only have what funds you sent. Keep all of this a secret, okay? If you love me, you will."

I responded: "That's probably right about the cost of the ticket now, but I am concerned about those boxes of gold passing through customs in those four airports. Murphy's Law is anything that can happen will happen."

July 25, 2018, at 9:10 p.m., Steve Cryer <Hangouts> "Janet, you treat me like a kid. I can do this. Your man is strong."

I was so excited and wanted to share this development with my friend Mary Ann, but I suppressed the thought. I'd shared a few things about Steve with her, but her reply to this scenario would indeed be how unlikely he would ever be with me, and I didn't want to hear it. She probably thinks no one would be interested in me. I feared she would judge me, and if Steve and I didn't work out, I'd be humiliated. So instead, I focused on the thought of picking Steve up at the Detroit airport, where I would proudly drive my man to the bank, the first place he would go after arriving on US soil!

8: THE VICTIM

Late July 2018.

> *"If you can trust yourself when all men doubt you, but make allowance for their doubting too—you'll be a man, my son."*
>
> *—Rudyard Kipling*

I probably should call or send a message to the kids. I haven't talked to any of them in several days. I know they're busy with their families and work. But, what will we talk about! I haven't done much this week, at least nothing I'd be willing to share with them.

My family didn't have much opportunity to see my anxious behavior. They were busy with their daily lives. I attended some of the grandchildren's ball games and dance recitals but exited immediately afterward, so I could minimize their scrutiny. My daughter Susan was on my Chase bank account and could have seen the $5000 transfer to Seth's account. I worried she would check into it, but she hadn't questioned me up to that point. Sitting at the computer with my cell phone by my side, I wait for an email or text from Steve. Even a "Hi, Honey, how are you? How are the cats? Have you eaten?" will excite me. So I'll play solitaire on my trusty computer until I hear from him.

***

Two days after Steve's departure from Dubai and on his long journey to the US, he texted me that he was having trouble in customs in the city of Accra, Ghana, Africa. He and his gold had arrived successfully at this first stop of the journey, but they detained him upon his arrival. The Ghanan officials demanded testing to ensure no viruses were coming into the USA from inside the containers. He needed my help. My cell phone rang.

July 27, 2018, at 8:10 p.m., Steve Cryer <No caller ID> "I'm in trouble! I'm afraid the police will arrest me and take the gold. They're all over the airport. I'm so scared..."

The muscles in my hand went weak, and it was difficult to hold the phone as I strained to listen to the voice on the other end of the line. I could barely understand the man. His speech was garbled, and his voice was high-pitched and loud. He repeated himself several times, "I'm in trouble. I'm afraid."

This was the first time I heard Steve's voice. My first thought was— it sounds like he's speaking with an African accent. I was frightened and I hung up right away. For three months, I'd longed to hear Steve's voice, the voice of the sweet man behind the computer screen. But when I heard this, I was shocked and so disappointed. Is he African? This person I'm talking to right now can't be Steve! He yelled at me! I didn't think Steve would ever raise his voice to me. This must be someone else. Did Steve have someone else call me, someone better at acting crazy? The phone rang again. I let it ring five or six times.

Finally, I said: "Hello."

July 27, 2018, at 8:20 p.m., Steve Cryer <No caller ID> "I'm in trouble! The police are watching me! I'm so scared! Will you help me?"

It was the same crazy-sounding voice, and I wanted to tell him this was his problem now. But, instead, I listened a few minutes to his tirade without saying a word and then hung up. What could one say to this garbage?

I reeled in shock after that interaction. The voice was not what I had longingly anticipated from the sweet man I'd come to know. His texting had always been cheerful, calm, even funny at times. Instead, this man on the phone was so angry and afraid, and I could barely understand him. What struck me was the tone, and it sounded like an insane lunatic. It was damn frightening!

After that, I didn't accept Steve's phone calls or text messages for a few weeks. I thought seriously of putting this whole mess behind me, moving on with life, and forgetting Steve. This phone call had shocked me to the core. It was painful to abandon the hope he would want me as much as I did him, but the man sounded hysterical. My friends knew something was bothering me and probably noticed I was conflicted. I tried to keep up my real life, socializing with my few friends and attending Mass every Sunday.

Now, addicted to my phone and Steve's constant attention, the gadget was my constant companion. Even though he'd stopped calling when I ignored him, the device was like a security blanket. It was in my pocket or nearby at all times.

My motto had always been to hold firm to my commitments. If I make a decision, I stick to it and helping Steve was one of those. But after the bizarre call, I did have the nagging thought twirling around in my head that Steve might be a fake. That rant I'd listened to scared me, and fear is an effective motivator.

***

One day I lost my fight against the urge to call Steve. "How are you doing?" I texted on August 30th.

August 30, 2018, at 8:10 p.m., Steve Cryer <Hangouts> "Shitty. What did you think? I've spent the last five weeks here in Accra, waiting for someone to help me. And you won't even talk to me. I told you I would pay you back every cent I get from you. I know you have money."

I said: "All you want is my money."

August 30, 2018, at 8:12 p.m., Steve Cryer <Hangouts> "Honey, I told you I'd repay you as soon as I get home. But, after sleeping in the airport a few nights and dodging the police officers, I got lucky. I met an airport police officer who sympathized with me, named Martin. He's a nice Christian man and he took me to his own house. He's letting me stay there in a spare room. I ride back to the airport each day with him, so that I can check on the gold. It's kept in a locker there in the airport, but they're charging me $100 a day for storage."

I replied: "That's nice you've found a friend. I'm happy for you."

August 31, 2018, at 7:10 p.m., Steve Cryer <Hangouts> "Janet, these bills are adding up every day I'm here in Africa. I feel like a beggar taking food and a room from Officer Martin and his wife. I'm embarrassed and depressed."

He continued to remind me of the accumulated bills and started pushing, saying he needed money: daily storage and fees for testing the gold and room and board at Martin's.

September 1, 2018, at 1:00 p.m., Steve Cryer <No caller ID> "You know, I can see your bank account, and I know you have $20,000 and spent $100 this morning."

Shocked at hearing his voice and his comment, I responded, "I don't believe you can see my account, but I'm happy to hear your voice when you're not yelling at me." *I have more than $20,000 in my Credit Union account, but I haven't purchased anything on that card for two days. He's bluffing! Finally, I get to hear his normal voice. I'm not happy with what he's saying about my bank account. But, I've been waiting for months to be able to talk to him.*

September 1, 2018, 1:10 p.m., Steve Cryer <No caller ID> "I have a marriage certificate showing you and I are married too."

I responded: "How the hell did you get that?" I'd like to see this document, even though I know it's fake.

September 1, 2018, 1:15 p.m., Steve Cryer <No caller ID> "You can get anything on the internet, Baby, lawyers will do anything for money."

I was pretty sure this man couldn't get an authentic marriage document nor see my bank accounts, but this scared the crap out of me. My chest tightened, and I felt weak all over. What if he can?

September 1, 2018, 1:20 p.m., Steve Cryer <Hangouts> "Even though I can see what you have in your accounts, and I could get access to the money, I didn't, and I never would do that. You trust me and I don't want to break our trust."

I immediately checked my bank account activity online, and there were no unusual transactions. I wanted to ask for details, and was almost certain Steve was lying, but not 100% sure. So far, I had only given him the $5000 to get out of Dubai and purchased the birthday computer for Selina, so if we separated, I was only out that much. Maybe it was time to take a break from Steve Cryer, even if I was often tempted to contact him?

I shared the basic facts of this relationship with my friend Mary Ann, and she was primarily supportive. She knew I met Steve online, had been texting him for a few months, and that he was working in Dubai but couldn't get back to Michigan. She was a widow and understood loneliness. I didn't tell her anything about sending him money, though. One day she asked me to watch an episode of "Dr. Phil," which featured an interview with a woman who had lost several thousand dollars in a Nigerian dating scam. I didn't want to tune in as my situation was much different. I watched a few minutes of it, only to appease Mary Ann. *That isn't me. I knew what I did was risky and probably unwise, but Steve didn't coerce or force me to give him money, like the woman on TV. I was freely choosing to help my friend.*

I returned to the dating sites and chatted with other guys, and I'd almost forgotten Steve. Then, about a month after my last contact with him, I happened to check my new Gmail account. There was an email from Selina waiting for me.

September 23, 2018, 3:10 p.m., Selina Cryer <Selina30K> "You're the reason my Daddy is dying." I felt her anger towards me and frustration at being unable to do anything about it.

I texted Steve. "Hello."

September 23, 2018, 3:15 p.m., Steve Cryer <Hangouts> "You're the last person I thought I'd hear from."

I wrote: "What's going on?"

September 23, 2018, 3:18 p.m., Steve Cryer <Hangouts> "This idiot found me and took me to the hospital. I've been treated for four days and got discharged yesterday. I was ready to die, had nothing to live for. I was in Ghana, scared for my life, and wanted it to be over. And you abandoned me, my only hope of getting out of here.

I texted him. "I want to talk to you on the phone." *In this situation, asking for help again, he'd better talk to me.*

September 23, 2018, 4:10 p.m., Steve Cryer <Hangouts> "My throat hurts a lot, and I can't say much. I took a lot of pills. Officer Martin found me in the bedroom on the floor, unconscious."

I replied: "How could taking pills make your throat sore and affect your voice? Who found you? Where were you? I need to talk to you, so call me."

September 23, 2018, 4:35 p.m., Steve Cryer <No caller ID> "Hello, why did you want to talk to me? I'm in pain." His voice was raspy, and he spoke very slowly and deliberately.

I said: "I think I deserve to get a real call from you, to hear your voice, now that I know you're able to use your phone over there. I was so shaken up when I first heard your voice. You sounded crazy, shouting and crying like a mad man! I didn't want to hear from you again."

September 23, 2018, 6:16 p.m., Steve Cryer <No caller ID> "Janet, I was so scared. Now I can't talk." *He does sound bad, so I guess I'll let him go. But, at least he did what I asked and called me.*

I wrote: "Selina sent me an angry message. She thinks I am to blame."

September 23, 2018, 6:30 p.m., Steve Cryer <Hangouts> "Selina has refused to go to school and said she wants to die."

This was a lot to digest! Selina's grandparents should get her to a doctor if she talks suicide. Steve should demand they take care of her. There's medication for depression, and it's the adults' responsibility to see to it she gets it. So why is he telling me this anyhow?

September 23, 2018, 7:10 p.m., Steve Cryer <Hangouts> "I can't bear to talk to Selina on the phone because of my voice. It would scare her."

I wrote: "I think you're mistaken. Call her." *I think any girl would appreciate hearing her father's voice, no matter how it sounded. He must be a mess emotionally. He just tried to kill himself! He's probably very unstable. If I ever do get to meet and be with him, I'll be looking for signs of anxiety or depression. But I can handle it! I've dealt with worse things in my life. When he gets home, I'll support him and get him to doctors and therapists.*

I asked Steve for Officer Martin's email. They had gotten very close while Steve lived with Martin's family in Accra, Ghana. Martin wrote to me shortly afterward.

RISING FROM DECEPTION

From: Martin Willson <martinjob1947@gmail.com
Subject: About your husband
To: Janet Marshall
Date: 23 September 2018

Dear Madam: I just got word back from Customs they tried reaching you about Steve illness but you changed your number and is not going though. Anyway there is bad news he could not stand loosing you so took in some pills to kill himself, because he felt it was too much on him and he was rushed to the hospital.

But I finally got a letter from his lawyer in Germany stating he wanted to send you an email. He needed your email to do the rest of the paperwork incase Steve don't make it. He ask them to send all his money to you to take care of Selina. So incase you get an email this is going on. He instructed me not to ask you for money to help him, but if he died he just want you to promise to take care of Selina.

This is the lil information I have for now. He already have your bank info so incase you get any money into your account it means he is dead and no more. They are still operating on him and I don't know his faith (fate) now. I wish and pray you and your husband didn't have to end this way to show him his last respect. I thought you both loved each other and you were a very strong woman. In all God bless you I'm just a messenger.

So Steve had money in Germany but couldn't get hold of it while he was in Ghana, and $3,000,000 in Detroit, also frozen? He claimed he needed to be there in person to withdraw from either of those accounts.

I wrote: "Steve, it is so hard to believe. Can't your lawyers in Germany bring you a portable facial and fingerprint recognition device, or get your signature notarized there in the hospital? You can't tell me a person of your means would need to ask for financial assistance from a woman like me, and someone you've never even met? And why does Martin refer to me as your wife? I am not."

September 23, 2018, 7:20 p.m., Steve Cryer <Hangouts> "I'll repay you double whatever you would lend me. Will you think about it? I love you, Janet."

Good Lord! I'm shocked. This man has money but can't get to it? He and Officer Martin talk about thousands and even millions of dollars. They must think those enormous numbers impress me. They don't, and I believe they're inflated or a lie. But I'm convinced he does need some help. I'll mull this over for a while before I answer.

I went to Mass that Sunday and prayed for a sign to help me decide what to do. The Gospel reading was about the widow giving her last cent to the poor. The phrase about giving her last cent to the poor that kept repeating in my head. I considered this to be MY SIGN. I would help Steve.

Sometimes, just one word or phrase will come into my head when I contemplate. I usually connect it to something in my life, but not always. It's frustrating when I don't know what it means. Who knows why I think those things? Sometimes when I'm reading or doing chores, a thought will come into my mind. I figure it's sort of A.D.D., attention deficit disorder, but it often leads me to do something I've been meaning to do but have forgotten. Like send a belated birthday card, put some item on the grocery list, schedule an appointment, look out the window at the moon, or research when the earliest snowfall of the year occurred.

The next day, I texted: "Steve, I've decided to do what I can to help you get home."

September 24, 2018, 9:10 a.m., Steve Cryer <Hangouts> "You're my savior, and I'd be dead if not for you. I'll give you some new directions on how to get money to me."

He had me hooked, but I felt like a frightened fish on a barbed hook. The charitable nature in me was burning, and I would do my best to get him home and wouldn't give up. I was shaking with excitement, believing the good Lord was behind me. I could get this man and his daughter back together, and this young girl could carry on with her daddy by her side. All my efforts would be worth it. Money's not everything, I rationalized. I considered this was like giving to a charity, and I knew who the money was going towards. *How much better can you get?* I knew deep down I might not get all of the funds back as he promised, but I didn't care at this point.

September 24, 2018, 10:10 a.m., Steve Cryer <Hangouts> "I'll get you an address for Seth, and you can send cash through the Post Office, rather than transferring money to his bank account. He's having trouble with the bank, and they're questioning why money is deposited, then transferred out of his account." *I suspect Seth works with more people than Steve, so his account might be very active and cause suspicion.* "The Post Office doesn't scan the envelopes, so they don't know what's inside. You need to get plain brown envelopes, put a magazine inside, and then slide small white envelopes with the money inside, in between the pages. $100 bills don't take up as much room as smaller bills. Send the envelope overnight and tell them the envelope carries documents. Don't take out any additional insurance as it could make them suspicious. Then, please take a photo of the receipt showing a tracking number, and text the picture to me."

Sitting on my couch, counting, sorting, and putting five $100 bills into each little white envelope became my task of the day. I was careful to stagger the seven small envelopes inside the magazine to keep the package from becoming bulky in any one place. My heart raced, and I'd hold my breath as I fingered those bills, but it was to ensure I was following the directions. I didn't consciously think about the dollar values. After I mailed this envelope containing $3,300 and texted the tracking information to Steve, I started breathing normally again. I realized I was excessively thirsty as I had overlooked meals and water consumption for a couple of hours. *It would be as easy as pie if I had to do this again. I'm experienced!* And soon, he would be in Michigan, and we could be together.

9: OUT OF AFRICA

....

*"The two most challenging tests on the spiritual road
are the patience to wait for the right moment and the
courage not to be disappointed with what we encounter."*

—*Paulo Coelho*

....

Steve continued to remind me that he'd be dead if it weren't for me.
Even though I knew it was subtle manipulation, it made my heart swell
with pride. It fulfilled my desire to help the unfortunate. He reminded
me I'd saved him from being stuck in Dubai without money after he'd
left his wallet in an Uber. I'd saved him from being arrested in the Ghana
airport, in the land he hated and feared for his life. He lamented, Africa
would be his last stop in life. He'd die there. But, I was his angel, saved
him after he took all the pills. I'd talked him through many a depressing
night too. His daughter and I frequently kept in contact, especially after
the pill ordeal. I wanted her to know her Dad was okay. So, he would
say over and over,

September 25, 2018, 7:30 p.m., Steve Cryer <Hangouts> "I owe you so much, Janet. I want to give you half of the gold bars."

I replied: "It is the devil's gold, Steve. I don't want ANY. It's caused you so much grief. You even told me once, you wished you'd not taken it at all, and had just come home."

September 25, 2018, 7:40 p.m., Steve Cryer <Hangouts> "You're such a strong woman. You don't let people tell you what to do. You make your own decisions."

Yeah! I'm strong. I've proved it so many times.

September 25, 2018, 7:50 p.m., Steve Cryer <Hangouts> "You're so smart too." He was impressed I volunteered at a museum and aided troubled youth, had an advanced degree, and was a teacher.

You're absolutely correct.

September 25, 2018, 7:55 p.m., Steve Cryer <Hangouts> "You're not greedy either. You don't even want any of the gold."

September 25, 2018, 7:58 p.m., Steve Cryer <Hangouts> "I can't wait to be together,... I want to spend the rest of our life together,... to grow old together."

It seemed I'd been feeling lonely for years, and this sounded fantastic. I thought I loved this man, even though I'd never seen him in person.

***

I woke up to a disaster in my house. The water coming out of my faucets and in the toilet at my forty-year-old home was pure black! We were in the middle of a drought in Michigan, and my pump had been laboring as I watered my newly seeded lawn day and night. So naturally, I complained to Steve about it.

September 28, 2018, 7:10 p.m., Steve Cryer <Hangouts> "Take a photo and send it to me. I want to see what you're talking about."

I did. *I bet he's shocked to see everything isn't so perfect in my life.*

September 28, 2018, 7:20 p.m., Steve Cryer <Hangouts> "When I get home, I'll help you fix the problem. I'm a handy man. You won't have to hire a man to do your jobs. I'm your man."

***

Steve shared what he knew about the internet cafes in Ghana. Going back and forth from the airport to Martin's house each day, he stated he passed by the cafes.

September 29, 2018, 1:10 p.m., Steve Cryer <Hangouts> "Scammers hang out in the cafes around the airport, and talk to women, either emailing or texting from their cell phones. They work in the afternoon, because they sleep all morning. In the late evening, the owners open up cafes for the scammers. The police leave them alone, and it works for them, with the eight-hour time difference between Africa and the states."

September 29, 2018, 1:20 p.m., Steve Cryer <Hangouts> "I even did it one day. I talked to a woman. The scammers gave me $200 for doing it. If I hadn't done it, they would've beaten me up or raped me. I never did it again, though."

I replied: "I'm shocked you got involved Steve, even for one day, and even more so that you told me about it. I can't imagine seeing this activity at all. It would disgust me, I think."

September 29, 2018, 2:00 p.m., Steve Cryer <Hangouts> "I fixed one of the airport guy's computers the other day, and he gave me $500 for doing it. I don't have any money so this is what I've been living on for these weeks."

I wrote: "Are you kidding, they'd let you touch their computers?! I know you are computer savvy. You've shown how you can attach video and audio files of love songs, and send them to me. I do enjoy all the songs we've shared though. Keeps me in a happy mood for some time. But surely, airport computers are password protected. You must be talking about someone's personal laptop. By the way, how do you pay for your cell phone and laptop computer? You seem to be able to communicate with me, even though you tell me you're without money."

It was the last days of summer now, and I longed for a man's touch. It had been so long since I'd held hands, hugged, or spent time with a gentleman. The warm weather and blooming plants in my flower beds temporarily boosted my morale as I walked around the yard every morning. I was blossoming like a flower, but still, I felt doubtful. Who could or would love me? This man had never even seen me in person. What were the chances he'd even like me when he did?

***

I advised Steve I would help him get out of Africa and come home. My mind kept returning to the Gospel reading about the woman who gave her last cent to the poor. He claimed it would take $8,000 to get his trunk of gold bars out of storage in the Accra, Ghana airport, $1,500 to pay for his plane ticket, which would be to Amsterdam and then Detroit, Michigan, $4,000 to pay his hospital bill for the four days he was hospitalized, and a couple of hundred dollars to Officer Martin for the room, board, and transportation. It took over a week for me to collect money. I closed out the account at one bank and cashed in some forty-year-old US Savings Bonds for a total of $15,000. I was so nervous but tried to appear relaxed and calm when I approached the bank tellers.

I shared with the tellers: "I'm planning on purchasing a new car. This winter, I need an all-wheel-drive vehicle to get me through the snow and ice. Last year I felt tied to my house when the weather got dicey. Living alone, I need to have dependable transportation." I knew from other experiences that keeping the conversation moving and providing a reasonable explanation for using the money would get the transactions done without too much questioning. Once I'd deposited all the money in my credit union account, I'd return home and initiate the

$15,000 transfer to Seth Jnr from my computer. Seth advised Steve he'd opened this new account in another credit union after Chase Bank froze that other account for some reason, and he forwarded that information to me. *Probably the same reason I had to send cash, sometimes the bank questioned his activity.* Once the funds showed up in the account, Seth would transfer them to Steve in Ghana. As Steve had vowed to get home as soon as possible, I went along with this plan.

September 29, 2018, 7:10 p.m., Steve Cryer <No caller ID> "Honey, I'm on my way home and will be out of Africa, where every day I was afraid for my life. Almost home on US soil! And we'll finally be able to see each other. I look at your photo every day and think of our future together. Like we talked before, we can write a good book soon."

I replied: "Steve, I feel more secure now that we have talked a few times on the phone. I'm convinced you're real now. I love hearing your spontaneous giggle—you have a contagious laugh. We'll write a book about our unique experiences."

While I had a few reservations now and then, we were both glad to see this ordeal concluding, and I was content to have been able to come up with the support he needed. Steve promised to text me when he boarded the plane on Sunday morning, September 30th.

It was the wee hours of the morning, and still in my pajamas, I waited for Steve's text to confirm he did board the plane and that it had departed Accra, which is in a time zone five hours ahead of Detroit. I was uneasy that my man might not be telling me something. But, as I was eager to see him face-to-face, I shoved those worries out of my mind. He told me that my voice made him smile, and those few times we did talk, I could hear his laughter over the phone.

So after a few hours and not hearing from Steve, I relented and contacted Martin. Working at the Accra airport, he claimed he had access to flight data. Martin sent a short reply.

RISING FROM DECEPTION

From: Martin Willson<martinjob1947@gmail.com
RE: Flight
To: Janet Marshall
Date: 29 September, 2018

He's listed as boarding.

September 30, 2018, 10:10 a.m., Steve Cryer <Hangouts> "I was in a rush and got seated on the plane just before take-off, so I didn't have enough time to text you. But I'm almost home, Babe. I used the onboard internet to text you. Can't wait to see you. I'll text or call you when I arrive in Amsterdam. It's a six-hour flight, and I have a five-hour layover there before I board for Detroit."

I replied: "It's hard to believe you would be running behind time for this long-awaited flight home. But at least now I know you're okay and on your way. Can't wait to see you."

Take a deep breath, Janet! *I can't dismiss this worry from my mind. I'm afraid he will be questioned, detained, or otherwise won't be allowed to fly.*

I set my cell phone down beside me on the couch, shut my eyes, and tried to breathe normally. I was exhausted, hungry, and torn between appreciative and apprehensive thoughts. After these last months corresponding with Steve, I couldn't wrap my head around the reality of him being home. This "project" of helping my man had consumed my life, but I worried it was a long shot and I might never see him at all. I had to believe he was honest, or I'd collapse. I prayed I could continue my support of this guy and get him home. But, I felt like I was on a runaway train, and the end of the tracks was a long way off, barely in sight.

10: REALITY PAYS A VISIT

October 2018

....

"Everything I ever thought has turned out different."

—Carmac McCarthy

....

On October 1st, I drove to the Detroit airport to retrieve my boyfriend. He successfully traveled from Accra, Ghana to Amsterdam, so I was confident he would make this last leg of his trip. He was leaving Amsterdam and arriving in Detroit that morning. I was excited, giddy over the first meeting with my handsome, blue-eyed virile man. Would he grab me and hug me, right there on the sidewalk, like he'd promised?

My drive to the airport was a distance of sixty miles one way. My outfit of a carefully selected colorful skirt and blue blouse had been lying on my bed for several days in anticipation of this day. I'd had one cup of coffee and a muffin when I left before sunrise and carried a couple of granola bars and bottled water in my car. I anticipated a substantial wait for this international flight to arrive. By my calculations, his plane should arrive about 7:00 a.m.

I was nervous as a schoolgirl, but my mood wavered as the minutes wore on. My breaths were shallow, and my stomach tightened as I checked and rechecked my cell phone over the two hours, from 7:00 a.m. to 9:00 a.m., for a possible missed call from Steve. Why doesn't he call me? I began to feel nauseous and troubled while sitting in my car in the international arrivals lot. I couldn't leave the car as it surely would be ticketed or towed away. Exhausted and now filled with doubts, a text finally came in.

October 1, 2018, 9:10 a.m., Steve Cryer <Hangouts> "I was in line at the terminal in Amsterdam, ready to board, when I heard my name called over the loud speaker telling me to step aside. They said I hadn't paid the storage fees for the gold in Ghana. I'm so upset."

I wrote: "You paid those charges with my money! The airport clerk accepted $2000 for shipping your packages, and you told me he posted it on the outside of the box, "Paid in Full." Steve, didn't you ask for a receipt? The clerk stole your money and you have no proof you'd already paid it!"

What the hell! Who would be so complacent as to forget to ask for verification after handing over $2000? Ghana is a developing country with significant government and police corruption. We see it in the news. After protecting the gold and making plans with Officer Martin, wouldn't he have anticipated this possibility? I couldn't believe the man I yearned to meet was so dumb! It had taken several hours for him to let me know, all the while I'd been waiting in my car at the airport. This is just too much!

Staring at his text, "They wouldn't let me board the plane," I didn't think I had the energy to move, say nothing about the drive home. I felt like a wrung-out dishrag, disappointed beyond description. With pent-up anger, tears ran down my cheeks. I so wanted our relationship to come true. I wanted to believe. What was I to do next?

I was uneasy about sharing this disappointment with my friend, Mary Ann, but I needed to let someone know what had happened. I sat in my car, motionless, unclear of where I was, sweating but shivering, squeezing my eyes shut and trying to keep from shaking. Was I having a breakdown, a panic attack? After a couple of minutes, I opened my eyes, readjusted my vision, and sent a short text to Mary Ann. He didn't arrive, and I'm so disappointed. I was still in the cell phone lot. I thought to myself, I can't sit here forever, so I put the car in gear, and headed back north toward home. I'll stop at McDonalds and get a cup of strong coffee. I had to stay alert long enough to return to my refuge. I'll stay off the phone for the rest of the day. I can't bear to talk to anyone. I'm so heartbroken!

After the wasted trip to the airport, I isolated myself for several days and made excuses to avoid people. My refrigerator was bare, but I managed to find enough food to sustain myself. I needed to avoid confrontation with people, even strangers in the grocery store. For now, I had to insulate myself from comments which I would find challenging. "Where have you been? What have you been doing lately?" In these times, even well-meaning questions like these would cause me to get emotional. I'd desperately wanted it to be true that I'd found a man who loved me, wanted to be with me and shared my dreams. I believed I loved him.

The next day, I notified Officer Martin of Steve's situation. Martin contacted someone he knew in the Amsterdam airport, and they found a nearby hotel room. This way, Steve didn't have to hang out in the airport while figuring out a solution to his problem.

I'd heard this sad story from him before, of things going awry, and had sympathized. I'd sent him money to solve those problems and help him get home. Still, on this day I sat all alone.

On October 2nd, I wrote: "Maybe you could try buying marijuana, It's legal in Amsterdam." *I can try to distract him from his situation, cemented to his room in the Netherlands. If I were stuck there, I'd do something!*

October 2, 2018, 5:10 p.m., Steve Cryer <Hangouts> "I don't smoke weed, and why would you even mention that to me? I don't even go into the city."

I responded: "Ok, it was a thought. But, you told me you don't drink alcohol, so I guess you wouldn't use any drugs either."

Officer Martin's emails came several times per week now. He told me how unfortunate the "good man" Steve was and that he was scared to ask anyone to help him. Martin had promised he wouldn't ask me for any help. Besides providing food, a room, and a daily ride to the airport, I don't think anyone other than Martin has helped Steve. Martin claimed we were a good match and believed Steve would propose marriage someday. *Either I'm naive, gullible, or just generous, but I'm the only one who has helped poor Steve.*

Martin shared that he and Steve talked about keeping me safe from scammers when he got home. *Maybe I'm a mark for all the swindlers out there? Is that what he's alluding to?* Martin advised I needed to be careful, as scammers were organized and deceitful. During these days of waiting for someone to come to his aid, Steve shared what he knew about scammer teams. He said he didn't want to scare me, but I should be aware and alert myself.

October 4, 2018, 7:00 p.m., Steve Cryer <Hangouts> "Janet, I'm not a scammer or part of a scamming team. My Army buddy, Seth Asamoah, is an ex-agent who investigates scammers. I've told him to never take money from your account, nor do anything to scare or harm you. I know some scammer teams are very organized. They have writers who create the profiles on the dating sites, and they write love letters to the woman. There are researchers who find out where the woman lives, connects to her bank accounts. They can clone her computer and watch her phone activity. There are mules, people who move money around the world for them. Their team might live around the world, maybe in the UK, USA, Australia, Maylasia, Germany, Nigeria, Ghana, and other places. They share proven methods on how to connect with a woman too. But, I'll never let anyone hurt you."

Officer Martin forwarded several videos to me. One was an arrest of three dark-skinned African men, escorted from a house in handcuffs in what appeared to be a run-down African village. The arresting officer was a white man, and he spoke German or Dutch, it seemed to me. He was yelling at the arrested men, and the villagers were all around, watching the event. Another video was of an undercover agent, a white man, in a small bedroom talking with two young twenty-something African men. He had a hidden camera filming this conversation as the boys freely talked about their "job." They were each sitting on a small bed with a laptop computer in their laps, and I could hear their conversations with women. I heard one say, "Baby, I love your tits. Show me more. No, you can't see me, my camera's broken." I saw silver duct tape over the camera lens on his computer, and he kept his eye on his screen. The agent questioned the boys about their endeavor to scam money from women and men. "Why do you do it?"

One young man said: "It's easy, and these people have lots of money. The white man owes us for taking us into slavery. And it's not really money. It's just on the internet. We aren't hurting anyone."

These videos sure appear to be real! Is he sending this to prove how I need him, that scammers might target me without his protection?

I texted Steve. "Martin sent me some videos. I couldn't believe what I saw. How could these boys scam money from women who were falling in love with them?"

October 5, 2018, 5:10 p.m., Steve Cryer <Hangouts> "I told Martin not to send those to you. I knew you would be afraid when you saw them. I wanted to wait till I was home and could be with you when you saw them. Then I could explain what was happening on the screen."

I replied: "What difference would that make?"

October 5, 2018, 5:15 p.m., Steve Cryer <Hangouts> "I want you to know, I will do everything I can to keep you safe. I've told my ex-agent friends to watch over you too. They do what I say. They know your account information and will watch to see that no scammers touch your money. You're safe Baby. Don't worry."

I hope this man, Steve, isn't a scammer himself. He seems to care about my welfare. He explains the workings of scammers. That's comforting. But, he seems unable to stay out of trouble and always needs help, often financial. Otherwise, I guess he hasn't hurt me.

***

Steve declared several times he would ask me to marry him when he got home. He said he'd wait for when the time was perfect. Even if I said, "No," he would keep trying, and until then, we could be best friends, soul mates.

I told him I would have to get to know him before considering a marriage proposal. He spoke of the marriage certificate to help him ship his gold to my house. Officer Martin often wrote to me about being husband and wife and being happy together. Living with Steve for those weeks, he wrote that the man was so happy when talking about me.

October 8, 2018, 9:10 p.m., Steve Cryer <Hangouts> "Would you ever marry a black man?"

I quickly responded: "Well, Steve, today I'm not in the marrying mood." *What a shock, and so out of the blue. What's he thinking?* "Why would you ask? Were you thinking of a certain black man?"

October 8, 2018, 9:15 p.m., Steve Cryer <Hangouts> "Janet, I was thinking if you wouldn't marry me, maybe you would marry my friend Chris, and he's black."

I wrote: "I've never heard you mention Chris. Is he another guy that needs a good woman? Seems like some of your friends, like Seth Jnr, have had bad relationships where the woman took their money and left them. I'm only interested in you." *I don't have the guts to ask Steve if he's black? He doesn't sound like it on the phone. But, this would be the time to ask. Would he tell the truth or lie? Either way, I still won't know for sure. I'm starting to think it wouldn't make a difference anyhow. It's the person inside I care about. I should probably ask him if the photos are really him, but I can't bear hearing they are not.*

October 8, 2018, 9:20 p.m., Steve Cryer <Hangouts> "I know we'll be married before one of us dies."

Why does he talk about death so easily? It makes me nervous. I'm too young to consider this happening. Maybe he speaks about it because he's faced his death.

I replied: "You talk about death too easily for me. It's not normal. And you're premature talking about marriage too. We need to get to know each other in person first."

Selina often talked about her dad and me getting married. I told her I hadn't even met her father yet. She claimed he regularly attended a Catholic church when he could and would probably join me once he was back home. Is she telling me this to increase the likelihood I'd marry her Dad? She shared the fact that her Dad could sing. Maybe he would sing for me sometime, she said. You should ask him.

Then I wrote: "Selina says you attend church when you can. Would you join me when you return to Michigan? I would so much like to have you sitting next to me in the pew. She says you sing pretty well. Will you serenade me tonight?"

October 8, 2018, 9:25 p.m., Steve Cryer <Hangouts> "Maybe when I get home and am by your side, I'll hold you tight in my arms and sing sweetly in your ear. You will like it."

I'm sure I will, Mr. Steve Cryer. So get your butt in gear and do that!

11: LIAR FOR HIRE

November 2018

....

*"I know God's doing all this to show
me something and tell me something."*

—Unknown

....

Steve had been stranded in Amsterdam for a month now, waiting for someone to come to his aid. He claimed he needed 8,000 to pay bills. We texted now and then in October, but I didn't commit to helping him.

November 14, 2018, 10:30 a.m., Steve Cryer <Hangouts> "Janet, what do you have planned for today?"

I replied: "Well this is Wednesday, and I'm doing laundry. It's too cold to go outside unless I need to."

November 14, 2018 10:35 a.m., Steve Cryer <Hangouts> "I'm so depressed. I can't wait to get out of here."

I wrote: "Maybe you think of other ways to get funds, but it doesn't seem that way to me. 'Get Janet to pay' is all I hear." *I complain to him, but I still wrangle with my decisions to give him the money he claims he needs! It's so hard* *to cut him off! I'll send him $8500 this one last time. Then he won't be able to say I kicked him to the curb when he was down and out.*

November 14, 2018, 9:25 p.m., Steve Cryer <Hangouts> "If I had other people to help me like u think, I will never ask u to help me. I swear to God I will never take any advantage over u I love u."

I said: "When Martin writes to me that WE need to work very hard to get the funds to allow your freedom, he means me."

November 14, 2018, 9:30 p.m., Steve Cryer <Hangouts> "Martin don't even have those thoughts for u. Martin don't even know the kind of money u have. Is my anti-scam group who knows all about your doing, and I haven't even said a word to Martin about your finances, so don't ever think he think u are rich, he rather think u taking loans from bank. Also I want u to know that there is no way I think u are a money machine, but there is one thing I know for sure, that is why I don't get scared when u helping, which is I know even if you give me one million US dollars, I can still pay u because I know I'm rich and have the money. I know God is doing all this to show me something and tell me something."

"You're absolutely right, Steve. I think about that all the time. What is God trying to show me, and to show you? Whatever that might be, I believe the right thing is very often the hardest thing to do." *I can't believe he said that. "God is trying to tell me something." I say that to myself all the time. But, with this unsolicited comment, I have a tiny hope he does have a conscience. Maybe he will turn around and make right all his promises?*

***

Officer Martin arranged for a Ghanan shipping company to get all the documentation necessary for US Customs. He sent me copies of those documents. *Republic of Ghana Ministry of Mines, in Accra, Ghana. A Certificate of Origin, Beneficiary: Steve Cryer.* He sent a copy of a letter from

Ghana Customs Excise and Preventive Services showing that Steve owned the gold.

I wrote: "Steve, Officer Martin has been very busy. He's gone above and beyond the call of duty as a good friend, and located documents you'll need."

November 28, 2018, 7:25 p.m., Steve Cryer <Hangouts> "Officer Martin is very particular and likes to do everything properly, so there won't be problems down the road."

Martin sent the shipping documents to me via email. Still, I noticed a few irregularities: a couple of misspellings and punctuation errors. Also, the fonts were not all the same on a document. Maybe officials in Ghana weren't as careful as Americans about expecting flawless documents?

***

Martin's wife, Janet (isn't that name interesting), needed to undergo emergency surgery. Martin was supposed to take her to Germany for the procedure and would be gone ten days. Steve claimed Janet would have a kidney removed and afterward would need some recovery time back in Ghana. In my research, I learned harvesting human organs and selling them in Africa, Malaysia, and Sri Lanka is a lucrative means of making a fast buck. Kidneys are most often harvested, as a person can live with one kidney. On the black market, one kidney can go for as much as $120,000. Would these guys be involved in this type of human trafficking?!

***

Officer Martin and Steve Cryer decided to ship the trunks of gold from Amsterdam to New York JFK airport. They claimed New York was a port of entry for gold and diamonds, and Detroit was not. After clearing

JFK, the gold would be loaded aboard another plane to Detroit. The boxes were addressed to Steve at my address. *It seems simple enough, but these guys have a history of forgetting some essential steps, causing the situation to go sideways.*

Martin sent me two videos, of men as they stacked the gold bars in a metal trunk, and the closed and locked trunk with my address boldly printed on it.

I wrote: "Steve, the video Martin sent showed someone packing the box with gold bricks. He was a bare-footed black man in khaki shorts. Really, are those two-kilogram blocks of gold? It kinda looks like bricks from my house sprayed with gold-colored paint. And is Martin a very dark-skinned man?"

November 29, 2018, 8:00 p.m., Steve Cryer <Hangouts> "Yes, he's Ghanaian and they tend to be dark. You worry about things too much. You know I will love u till the end of the world. I don't care about money if that is what you think, all I care about is my freedom and peace. If you could lend me just a little more, I'll be able to come home to you very soon. I'll text you a new Chase account, Patricia D. She's helping Seth Jnr now, as his bank and credit union have put holds on his accounts. Are you able to send another $8,000?" *I can make bank transfers to this woman from my computer, making it pretty easy. Maybe too easy? When Steve says he'll love me till the end of the world, I laugh because he gets common phrases turned around, but it gives me a nice feeling inside anyhow.*

"Steve, I'll make the $8k transfer this week."

The plan was when Steve arrived in Detroit, and I would reunite with him outside the International Terminal. It would be the first time we'd see each other, but the second time I'd gone to the airport. I'm sure there would be a few hugs and kisses, tears, and uncomfortable conversations, but hopefully, that would subside very soon. Then I'd drive him to his Bank of America there on Griswold Ave., and he'd withdraw the necessary funds from his account, which he claimed had a

$3,000,000 balance. Then we'd return to the Detroit Customs Office in the airport and pay the shipping charges of $20,000, and he'd be free. He would be using his own money! Waiting for all this to come to fruition, I busied myself with holiday preparations.

***

Christmas alone. I invited my children and their families to my house for Christmas Day dinner. I liked to put out a lovely table with all the linens and fine china at least once a year. The turkey was in the oven the night before at a low temperature. My daughters would provide the side dishes. There was a little snow on the ground this week, but the weather was quite warm. Everyone had arrived, and I was about to put the food on the table when I received a call on my cell phone, which was snugly hidden in the pocket of the apron I was wearing. I checked to see who it was and saw Steve's "No Caller ID" showing on the screen. So I hustled outside to the garage to take the call in private.

I said: "Hello. It's Christmas Day. Thank you for calling, Steve."

December 25, 2018, 1:00 p.m., Steve Cryer <No caller ID> "I wanted to say Merry Christmas, and let you know I'm thinking about you and hope we can be together very soon. What will you have for dinner?"

We chatted for a few minutes. It warmed my belly to have my boyfriend call on Christmas Day. Yet, I was anxious that my family might ask me questions about the call that had delayed the dinner.

When I quietly reentered the house, I noticed my children looking at each other, eyes rolling, and one sarcastically said, "What kind of emergency was that? Who was on the phone?"

"Oh, it was someone I've been talking to and he called to wish me a Merry Christmas. That's all." With this, I put an end to the questioning. "Let's pray and eat, and the food's getting cold."

***

January 8, 2019, 1:00 p.m., Steve Cryer <Hangouts> "Honey, I just boarded here in Amsterdam. I can't wait to be on US soil and see you, my Queen. Look for me: I'm wearing white Nike sneakers, khaki pants and white Polo shirt."

For the second time in a couple of months, I waited at the Detroit airport to meet my man. While in the pickup lane, Steve called from a phone he'd borrowed.

January 9, 2019, 12:50 p.m., <1-248-2xx-xxxx> "Janet, I have a problem. I can't come outside." *Why is he calling from this strange number?*

Steve had used the expensive airline ticket he'd purchased with my money. But, he informed me that once he arrived at the Detroit airport, customs officials wouldn't allow him to leave the airport to assemble the necessary funds to pay off his $20,000 debt to the Ghanian shipping company. He said I shouldn't come inside and claimed it wasn't safe. After he'd disembarked, the officers had confiscated all his luggage and his cell phone. He said he couldn't leave due to a hold initiated by the shipping company. But he was in the Detroit airport! I believed he was being held there. Why wouldn't I?

January 9, 2019, 1:00 p.m., <1-248-2xx-xxxx.> "Honey, if they see you, they might detain you too, hoping you'd pay the bill. You're not safe in here."

I replied: "I don't care. I'm coming inside anyhow. I'm not going to let you get this close and then just drive away."

I was troubled. I was within a few yards from being able to see my man for the first time. Safety be damned. I sat there for a while, trying to figure out how to get inside the terminal, to sneak a peek at this man. I've got to get inside and try to see him! I couldn't leave my car in the pick-up lanes, so I drove around the loop again, trying to think clearly. Maybe there was a place near the terminal doors where I could temporarily park the car for even a few minutes? I knew that terminal reasonably well as I'd traveled abroad several times in the last few years. *I think the Customs Office is close to the outside doors. I can almost see the area from the car.* But, I was afraid to get my car ticketed or towed, and maybe I was scared to learn that Steve was not there, and to admit defeat. The finality of that would be heartbreaking. So, I began the drive home in deep despair. I texted Mary Ann that I was coming home alone. After this terrible experience, as far as I was concerned, Steve could sit in the airport forever!

January 9, 2019, 3:00 p.m., Steve Cryer <Hangouts> "The customs officer here in Detroit told me I have seventy-two hours to pay the charges or they'd send me to JFK airport. He returned my cell phone, and I'm sitting here waiting for your help." *I guess they're sending him to New York City as that's where his gold is. I'm so mad at myself for not going inside that terminal. Then I would know if Steve was real or not!*

January 12, 2019, 1:00 p.m., Steve Cryer <Hangouts> "Janet, this morning the officers dumped me on a plane to JFK. I'm in New York City now, sitting in the customs area. I don't know what to do."

12: NO-SHOW

January 2019

....

"I love to travel, But hate to arrive."

—Albert Einstein

....

January 13, 2018, I wrote: "So your girlfriend didn't come through for you? What if I had brought the $20K to you in Detroit? How would that have worked? Would I hand over two-hundred Ben Franklins to some officer, ask for a receipt and then lead you by the hand out of the custom's area? Not very plausible! So, it's been three days now, and without their money, they sent you as far from Michigan as they possibly could? I don't blame them. JFK is a big airport, and that's where your gold is, so you'll be together, you and your precious metal. Maybe you can hide out until someone comes through and pays your fines? It'd be improper for you to ask me for more funds, considering how I've already given you a lot of money, and was inconvenienced at the airport two whole days." *I think it's a dumb idea to ship the gold from Ghana to NYC when Steve's destination is Detroit. But they say it's because New York is a port of entry for gold and gems, and his box needs to be checked out there before it can go continue, like to Detroit and finally my house. Even if I don't give him any more money, I do feel like I'm trapped in his net. Don't even know what I'm doing sometimes.*

January 13, 2019, at 11:00 a.m., Steve Cryer <Hangouts> "My prayer is to be with you forever. My love for you is deeper than you can imagine. I will always love you sweetheart. I want to always be by your side. You complete my world. Please help me get out of here and home to you."

I replied: "Steve, this is the same story I've heard from you before. You get in a jam and need money to get out of it. And it seems you always ask me to help you. Don't you have other friends?"

January 13, 2019, at 11:10 a.m., Steve Cryer <Hangouts> "Honey, I will forever be your guardian and will make sure you never lack for anything on earth. I've told you that I will repay you every penny you've spent on me. Isn't that enough?" *So where does he come up with these lines: lack for anything on earth?! And be my guardian? Maybe I do need one? I get so turned around in my mind, and make dumb moves.*

I said: "Steve, I'm getting bored. I need to move on, get a real boyfriend who can be with me and wants to be with me. You're making this a miserable experience."

***

February 14, 2019, at 11:00 a.m., Steve Cryer <Hangouts> "Happy Valentines Day, Sweetie. I can't wait to get home and squeeze you and kiss you." *Wow, this is out of the blue. I haven't heard from this guy in a month. At least he knows when the holidays occur. If he's in the JFK airport like he claims, he probably sees advertisements for Valentine's Day.*

I replied: "It's been a month since I heard from you. I told you I was moving on."

February 14, 2019, at 11:20 a.m., Steve Cryer <Hangouts> "Officer Martin has been working for me in Ghana, and has gotten the gold shipping company to agree to accept half payment, or $10,000, and then I'll pay the balance after I am released from custody. If you could help me now, after I get home, I can go to a Bank of America and withdraw the full $20,000 to repay the shipping company, and all the money I owe you as well."

I replied: "That's nice that Martin is trying to negotiate for you. Unfortunately, I'm not interested in getting involved in your situation again."

February 17, 2019, 8:00 p.m., Steve Cryer <Hangouts> "Honey, did you see the songs I sent to you on Hangouts? I think of you almost every hour of the day. If you listen to these songs, you'll know how I feel about you and me. They say the words I would love to whisper in your ear."

I replied: "I love the songs. I'm in a nice mood when I hear them. Some are from artists I've never heard of. You really do have a wide range of music interests, like you wrote on your PoF dating profile. I wouldn't mind attending a concert with you someday. Would that be possible?" *I know this will never happen, but it's fun to fantasize.*

February 17, 2019, 8:20 p.m., Steve Cryer <Hangouts> "Absolutely! I would charter a plane. I have the money you know. Once onboard the plane I'd keep you firmly in my arms while we secretly kiss. *Westlife* (one of the groups he introduced me to) doesn't tour in America this year, but they do in Great Britain. You know they are the Irish boy's group who've recorded some of those songs I sent you. We can take a quick flight and see them in London. Check out the dates on the internet, OK? We can talk about it tomorrow."

I was upbeat with the thought of attending a concert with this man. He'd introduced me to another artist, Ed Sheeran from Ireland, and his song, *Perfect*. It was often broadcasted in the states on the radio, and I listened to the lyrics intently, all about finding a beautiful girl, imperfect but perfect for him. They spoke to me, telling me what Steve wanted me to know about his feelings for me.

***

I had a hard time believing Steve could hang out in an airport overnight for several days. But he always talked a good line and had details that sounded almost possible. But, I couldn't imagine he could exist without money or food, or his luggage? This unfortunate man's only thing with him was a backpack and his cell phone with a charger. It was so convenient that he always had his cell phone to call me and stay in touch with his friends.

I sent a message to Officer Martin that I wouldn't help to get $10k. I thought I could, but I'd changed my mind, I told him.

I'd tried to get the money he said he needed, but all my attempts had failed. This time the Credit Union fraud employee called me. She left two messages on my home phone, and I took some time returning her call. I knew what she might say. When I did call her number, she answered and spoke in such a sweet voice. I couldn't be rude, so I answered her questions about who was receiving the money, and why. When I talked it through with her, she persuaded me to cancel the order to transfer the funds. After that phone conversation, and for a short time, I believed Steve was a fraud and was scamming me.

February 19, 2019, 8:00 p.m., Steve Cryer <Hangouts> "Martin was angry. He said that you'd caused him to be embarrassed in front of the shipping company when he couldn't produce the funds that he said he could. They wouldn't accept partial payment either. He told me he was upset that he'd spent his own money and time on transportation to their office. And I've been crying all day. I'm so tired of being a bum and wandering around this airport."

It's about time that Martin spends a little of his own money on his new best friend. I can't get a grip on the image of anyone just wandering around an airport?

I responded: "I just can't come up with even the $10k you said you need. I'm sorry."

February 19, 2019, 9:00 p.m., Steve Cryer <Hangouts> "I bought some Jack Daniel's Whiskey, one of those little bottles they serve on the airplane. I have a big headache from crying. I am so upset that the shipping company reneged on their promise of accepting half-payment to release my gold. But, I don't blame you, Honey. You tried to help me, I'm sure. I'm gonna get drunk if I can."

Empathy for this man's situation, I imagined him tired and alone in the small airport bathroom. I knew he never drank liquor. We'd talked about that when he was in Ann Arbor, and he said he didn't frequent the bars or keep liquor in the house. That evening he called me on his phone.

February 19, 2019, 11:00 p.m., Steve Cryer <No caller ID> "I'm so tired from crying all day. I want to go to sleep and never wake up."

I heard the click of a metal door closing, and then a sound like a lock locking.

I said: "Babe, don't down the whiskey in one gulp. You're gonna vomit it all up, and it won't even do you any good. Instead of decreasing your frustration, you're gonna have a big stomach ache as well as headache."

My comforting words and maybe my low sensuous voice did affect him. We chatted quite a while, and I tried to make him laugh. Laughter is an effective medicine! It was about an hour before I could hear deep breathing, and obviously, he went to sleep, probably on his backpack in the airport's bathroom stall! *How helpful of me to sacrifice my sleep and stay with this man as he falls into a deep slumber.* I cared for his mental and physical health, as I would with any friend. I longed for Steve to be the man I'd spend the rest of my life with. I finally fell asleep all alone in my spacious bed.

One time, during our phone conversation, I heard a knocking on a metal door and a person speaking in a loud, frustrated voice. I surmised that someone asked to use the bathroom he "lived" in. He yelled something back at them that I couldn't quite understand, but it seemed that he was telling them to go away. Steve said he avoided airport police all during the day and checked back into the customs office each morning and night, as they required. He couldn't leave the terminal until he came up with the $20,000 for the shipping company debt.

I said: "I can't figure out how all this is possible, Steve. What did the customs officers figure you would do all day, while they're waiting for you to come up with the amount of money they required? Wouldn't they have put you in jail or something? You can't hover around the airport. This can't be true. You know, I could drive from Michigan to New York in nine hours. Then I could see with my own eyes if you were genuine, and that you were really there wandering around Terminal #2 as you said. How do you feel about that?"

How did I get to this point? How the hell did I go from texting for an hour while I drink my morning coffee to mailing him thousands of dollars in a plain brown envelope? Now I can't even remember some of the reasons he gave me for needing the money. I know I questioned him at the time and resisted a little, but eventually, I gave in and sent it anyhow. I do remember that he first asked for a small amount of money. Then, each time he needed more significant amounts. So why don't I know why I did all of that?

February 20, 2019, 8:00 p.m., Steve Cryer <No caller ID> "Janet, you would want to see me for the first time, in these smelly clothes, dirty and hungry? If that's what you need to do, come ahead. I am ready to face you. Then you can get me out of this God forsaken airport, and I can come home. But, I'm worried the officers will see you talking to me and want to stop you too. You won't be safe, but if you are determined to come, to humiliate me to see if I'm real, then I can't stop you."

I'd already spent a lot of money trying to get this guy home. I desperately wanted to know he was the person he claimed to be. If I could see him for a short time, I would know. Steve had been managing without spending money on a hotel this time, sleeping in the airport's family toilet. He told me he'd befriended a clerk at the Starbucks Coffee Shop. Her name was Janet, and she worked hard to support her two children. *Is everyone he knows a Janet? I imagine this lovely woman in the Starbucks giving him a coffee and bun, doing what she can to help. I can do the same, and it makes me feel good.*

I withdrew $10k from my retirement account and proceeded to send it to him.

***

Steve had now spent over a month in the JFK airport. He had been sleeping next to the toilet with his backpack as a pillow. I knew I was crazy to think this was possible, but he was so convincing with all the details. He washed his three sets of clothes in the sink and dried them on the stall walls at night. The officers had allowed him to take these other clothes out of his suitcases.

I wrote: "Is there anywhere in the airport you can pay to get a real shower? Your hair and beard must be long by now too."

February 21, 2019, 8:00 p.m., Steve Cryer <Hangouts> "No, Honey. But I do use the soap in the bathroom to wash my armpits, organs and I wash my body as well. Even with long hair I'm still handsome. Your man is strong. I'm thinking of going to a nearby hotel, spending the night and taking my bath and then come back. But I'm scared I'll get caught and be in trouble. All I feel right now is gratitude for your kindness. Thanks for always appearing at a time of need and I will make sure I stay loyal to you no matter what. You will forever be my Angel is a promise."

The honesty of his statement made me chuckle. I've never heard genitals called "organs." Kinda naive and appealing. I imagine him soaking in a bathtub. I could help him wash his hair and scrub his back. A sweet thought!

I had seriously thought about taking a road trip to New York to investigate Steve's story of living in JFK airport. I had a great GPS in my car. I could reserve a hotel room nearby the airport and then drive to Terminal #2 to find him. I even asked my friend Mary Ann if she would ride along with me, and being the supportive person, she agreed. If we didn't find Steve, we could have a lovely weekend touring the city. I probably would be so disheartened if that were the case. It would devastate me. Maybe I was 'chicken shit,' but I didn't follow through with the plan.

February 21, 11:50 p.m., Steve Cryer <No caller ID> "Honey, I think sometimes you don't believe I'm real. Or you think I've lied to you about things. I've always told the truth. If you talked to Selina's grandpa and asked him any questions you might have about me, would that convince you I am real?"

I had declined this offer previously, as I knew he could have someone pretend to be her grandfather. Still, tonight he asked again, as we had been in another argument about him being "real," I reluctantly agreed to take the call.

I said: "Tell me what his name and phone number is, so when he calls, I'll answer the ring."

February 22, 2019, 12:20 a.m., Steve Cryer <No caller ID> "His name is Alan White, and here's his number."

It was 1:00 a.m. my time. The phone rang. It was the expected number. Supposedly, Alan lived in Missouri, which is one hour behind me, or midnight for him.

He came on the telephone with a pronounced southern US accent and said, "Steve told me to call you." *I know that accent. Ray's family is from Kentucky, and I've heard it a lot.*

I had had only a few minutes to formulate my plan and questions, so I was a little flustered. All I could think to ask was, "Steve's daughter is Selina, and she lives with you?" Then I blurted out, "How tall is Steve?" I'm not a quick thinker at any time of the day or night.

"Yes, Selina lives with her grandma and me. I am 5'9", and he's about my height, I guess."

Steve's Plenty of Fish profile said he was 6'1". *So, grandpa, either you don't know how tall Steve is, or he's lied to me, or maybe, you're talking about another guy.* Alan went on to say he rented the house from Steve and that he was a real nice guy! *Ya, Steve makes Selina's grandfather pay rent. That's not very generous, being he and his wife take care of Selina. But these are his in-laws. Is that the difference?* Steve had woken grandpa up to call me at this late hour, so the older man apologized for not having a clear head. He claimed he was glad to talk to Steve's woman finally and that I had a friendly voice. I wasn't convinced this was Selina's grandpa, but he was American for sure with that pronounced accent. This eases my mind a little about everyone in Steve's circle being African.

February 22, 2019, 12:30 a.m., Steve Cryer <No caller ID> "Well, did he call you? Are you convinced I'm real now?"

I responded: "Steve, I never questioned if you were real or not. I question if you are who you say you are. That's different. The guy that called me is surely American. He had a southern accent that I'm all too familiar with. But, he didn't describe you all so accurately. He did say he rented the house from you where Selina lives."

Steve again attempted to convince me he was "real."

February 23, 2019, 8:00 p.m., Steve Cryer <Hangouts> "Could I send you a car to hold until I return to Michigan? In Missouri, my friend, Mark Hopper owes me $20k and doesn't have the money to repay me right now, but he has a car he could give me. It's only worth about 10K. Could I send the vehicle to you, a 2010 Toyota Corolla? Maybe you could store it in your driveway? Then I'd have a vehicle to run errands around town. I want to buy a new truck as soon as I can. It'd only be a week or so that you'd have the car. I promise."

I hated when people said, "I promise." When overused, it is so aggravating and seems dishonest. But, I agreed to allow Steve to store a car in my driveway for a couple of weeks. This idea was pretty exciting! I'm sure I had a massive grin on my face! I was coming closer to seeing the whites of this man's eyes and diving into them to learn all of his personality. "What kind of truck would you want? I could shop around for you."

February 23, 2019, 9:00 p.m., Steve Cryer <Hangouts> "You are the queen of my heart, and I want to grow old with you. I would probably want a Chevy or Toyota."

"Steve, this is the Big Three territory. You'll want to get a GM, Ford or Chrysler vehicle."

In Michigan, we often have snow till Easter. Still, a little snow on the ground in February couldn't prevent Steve from having the car delivered to me. The vehicle will be arriving the following Friday afternoon. Steve gave my cell phone number to the delivery company. I would receive a call to advise an accurate arrival time. In the meantime, I received a couple of strange texts from the truck driver.

I'll be your address 2:30 p.m. Please stay there.
mojesh skazat skoiko gross for this week
Text me please
Sorry, wrong numb.
Can you call me 217-567-8900
What car you waiting?
Sorry, I have 2 more hr.

I didn't respond to the messages but right away checked the translation of the second foreign text as it was Russian. "Mojesh tell me how much gross for this week." This driver was texting someone other than me. I was now a little apprehensive about the delivery. What was happening?

Two hours later, I received another text from the driver: Madam, I'm stuck in the mud on Roseman Road near you. Do you know where this is?

I responded: "Yes, wait there. I'll come to you and lead you to my house." I found him quickly, like he said, stuck in the road. I rolled down my driver's side window, motioned to him to follow me, and slowly led him out of the mess. When we arrived at my house, I stopped my car at the end of the driveway, stepped out onto the road, and walked towards his truck. Staring at the guy as he leaned out the window, I gave him directions on parking on the road. It was a twenty-foot-long trailer attached to a big black Dodge Ram truck, and it couldn't make the sharp turn into my driveway. The blue Toyota was the only car on the three-car trailer.

The lone driver was amiable and spoke English well. I'd anticipated a strong accent based on the weird text I'd received earlier. He seemed nervous with me, as he rambled about getting lost and stuck in the road. I was alone at the house this day. Still, I sensed he was an experienced truck driver, and did this kind of thing all the time. I determined it was safe to let him disconnect the Toyota and park it in my driveway.

I said: "Where's your accent from?"

He replied: "I'm Russian, from the Georgian province. I live in Chicago with my wife and twin girls. I'd love to live in the country like this. My girls would enjoy playing in the field."

I said: "I'm sure your family would enjoy this part of Michigan."

He motioned and said: "Will you sign this I-pad? I can send you a copy of the receipt for the car. Here are two sets of keys and the vehicle title. Walk around the car and inspect for any dents in the body, the tires for tread ware, and any stone chips on the windshield."

I said: "Looks good to me. Is that all I need to do? There's no bill, right? Thank you and good luck in your travels." *I wonder how much it cost Steve and his friends to deliver this car?*

After the driver left, I cautiously unlocked the car door with the key provided, looked inside, and saw it was immaculately clean and smelled of bleach. I opened the trunk, and it was empty. What a relief! I texted Steve, "The blue car's now in my driveway."

I opened the driver's door, gingerly sat behind the wheel, inserted the key in the ignition on the steering column. I turned the key, and the motor fired up. I moved the gearshift to reverse, backed it up to park it slightly out of sight on the side yard. It only took a few minutes, so I exited the car, pushed the lock button down, shut the door, and hustled inside the house. I plopped down on the couch and tried to clear my head. *What had I done? Would this cause me any trouble? What would my children say?*

Steve called right away. February 27, 2019, 3:50 p.m., Steve Cryer <No caller ID> "Hello. So you have the car now?"

I replied: "Yes. I chatted with Dimitri a few minutes as we stood in my driveway. He took the car off his trailer and drove it up to my garage, as I asked. I was a little nervous being alone. Now I have a pretty blue car sitting in my driveway to remind me of you every time I look out the window. It's an older car, but It'll be good enough to get you around for the first few weeks. You'll be home soon, right?"

February 27, 2019, 4:00 p.m., Steve Cryer <No caller ID> "Yes, I'll do my best. Honey, thank you for being in my life. You are the reason I wake up every morning. I talked to Dimitri after he left your house. He said you were a friendly woman. I told him you were the 'real deal.' We use Dimitri and his company a lot for car deliveries."

I asked: "Steve, you talked to Dimitri?! How do you know the delivery driver here in the local area? How often do you need to use his company to move cars around? Did you know him when you lived in Ann Arbor? Why would you need to deliver vehicles or pick them up? Who is we? I don't understand. I'll expect you to explain every bit of this when you get home."

I looked at the vehicle title Dimitri had given me. Mark Hodder was listed as the owner, just as Steve had said. Otherwise, everything looked legitimate to me: Certificate of Title from State of Ohio, previous owner a dealership in Ohio, year, make, model of the car and purchase price. On the reverse side, Mark had signed off and dated it, just as one would expect.

Every day for the next few days, Steve reported to me he walked around the airport, trying to relieve his headache and keep himself occupied during the daytime, and exhausting himself so he might sleep a little each night. It seemed to me he was being a little paranoid, thinking others listened to our phone conversations, either people sitting near him or someone cutting into the phone call. When he became concerned like that, he told me he would call back later. *I wonder what this is all about?*

Sometimes, to wile away the time, he'd go to the Apple Computer store and play on the computers, he said. Or he'd watch television in the terminal, and he often watched the news on CNN. A few times, while we were chatting on the phone, he would ask me to, "Hold on, please." I then heard this unique but charming guitar music. At first, I thought he was playing the guitar for real, trying to impress me, and I commented on how I liked it. But then I realized he wasn't there at all, and this was a hold-on song. I figured it out when I noticed it looped a couple of times, and I heard the song repeated.

After a few minutes, he came back and said,

February 28, 2019, 5:00 p.m., Steve Cryer <No caller ID> "I'm sorry for keeping you waiting honey. That was Seth Jnr asking when I would be able to get money to him?"

I didn't respond to that question yet.

March 1, 2019, 1:00 p.m., Steve Cryer <No caller ID> "How is your day going? Hold on Janet. I need to help this guy solve his problem. He thinks another guy stole his jacket. No one here can solve their own problems, and they all come to me for my help."

I guess it sounds logical. If you're hanging around a place, you'll probably get to know people. But he's the one they go to for solving problems? Strange!

March 1, 2019, 1:20 p.m., Steve Cryer <No caller ID> "I'm back now."

I responded: "Who were your talking to, Steve? It didn't sound anything like English, and I heard you arguing with another guy."

March 1, 2019, 1:25 p.m., Steve Cryer <No caller ID> "The guy was one of the janitors in the airport I help now and then. I get bored so I grab a mop and wash a floor sometimes. The janitors here are my friends now."

I replied: "Good. I always say in my job it's been a benefit to get chummy with the janitors and secretaries. They know all the inside scoop and will do anything for you."

March 1, 2019, 1:35 p.m., Steve Cryer <No caller ID> "Great, but some people don't even respect them."

I said: "What language were you speaking with that guy? Judging from your tone, it seemed like something was wrong. Are you hiding something from me?"

March 1, 2019, 1:45 p.m., Steve Cryer <No caller ID> "What do you mean hiding something from you? I was speaking Dutch. What the hell did you think I was speaking? I speak four languages: English, French, German and Dutch. I can also understand the Ghanaian language but I can't speak it."

I said: "OK, Babe." I didn't want to aggravate him further. It wouldn't do any good.

These interrupted phone calls occurred several more times in the next few weeks, and sometimes I was on hold for several minutes. *Why do I let him treat me this way, putting me on hold for so long?* I sensed there was something else going on. After several of these cut-short conversations, I asked Steve if anything was wrong.

March 1, 2019, 1:55 p.m., Steve Cryer <No caller ID> "Yes. I didn't want to tell you."

I said: "You're acting like a little boy getting in trouble with Mom. Why would you hesitate to share with me? I'm not your Mom. Besides, you are no little boy. Tell me what's wrong."

13: TEMPER TANTRUM

March 2019

....

*"When you reach the end of your
rope, tie a knot in it and hang on."*

—*Franklin D. Roosevelt*

....

March 2, 2019, 1:25 p.m., Steve Cryer <Hangouts> "I didn't want to tell you, Janet, but the other day when I learned I wouldn't be able to leave New York and come home to you, I got mad. I pushed over the table in the customs office, knocking over their computer and ten other laptop computers stacked on the table there. They had to hold me back because I was so mad. The laptops are damaged, and I need to replace them."

I replied: "I don't even know what to say. You must have been acting like a madman to have broken ten laptop computers! Replace them? Why?" *How do you come up with these bizarre scenarios? If I were in my right mind, I would cut off all communication right now.* "Were they new in their original packaging boxes?! So you made that big of a mess all the while being held back by two officers?!"

What's he going to want from me now? It makes me sick to my stomach to think what it might be. He surely doesn't want my suggestions of what to do. I'll give them anyhow, and maybe I can delay the request, whatever it might be.

I wrote: "Go back and fix them. It's probably the boxes that are damaged, and all ten of the boxes can't be broken. This can't be true. You're exaggerating."

This story is total bullshit! I know it! I don't know why I don't flee this situation and forget this man. Somehow, I feel like I can't. It's similar to my less-than-perfect marriage. I won't give up. I'll be a quitter if I do. Once I make my mind up about something, I don't change it. If I stick by Steve, he'll know I care for him and come home to me?

March 3, 2019, 2:25 p.m., Steve Cryer <Hangouts> "Honey, don't treat me like a kid. U would have done worst if you were in my shoes. After I calmed down, I went back and dusted all the boxes off and could recover four of them. We only have to replace six of them. Can you help? Baby, please!"

I replied: "I notice you say "we." Who is the "we" you always refer to?" I wanted the "we" to be more than a business proposition. I longed to have this man as my partner.

March 3, 2019, 2:35 p.m., Steve Cryer <Hangouts> "I have had enough with explanations and you can choose to help or not. I won't be mad. Your man is strong! Everything was all busted up. I did calm down a little and then the officers told me I need to replace the ten computers and to do so before the boss gets back from his vacation, or I'll be put in jail."

Steve sent me a photo of a Mac Pro Computer, including the specifications. They were all the same, and each of them would cost $2500. *I sure would like a photo of the pile of broken ones.*

I wrote: "That's a costly laptop, Babe. I'd be thrilled to own one myself. Couldn't you have broken some cheaper ones?"

March 3, 2019, 3:25 p.m., Steve Cryer <Hangouts> "I hope you can help me. If you can, I need you to get these computers, in gray or silver would be okay. They need to be the same as the ones I destroyed."

I remember seeing these same computers in the video Martin sent me of the boys doing their scamming. They are the best that Apple Computers make. You can create movies, alter pictures, including documents, and the storage is a lot too. Is this coincidental?

I wrote: "You could probably fix those six computers you think should be replaced, as you repaired the airport employee's computer back in Ghana. Why not do that? If we do get replacements for those six, you could keep the damaged ones for yourself. I'm sure you're capable of repairing them and reselling them to get some pocket change for yourself."

I know he won't like this suggestion, and if he can fix them, where and how would he do that? But I want to give him some grief, as much as he's giving me. So I'll make him grovel a bit.

March 3, 2019, 4:25 p.m., Steve Cryer <Hangouts> "What the hell! I don't need to keep any damm laptops. What I need is my freedom. Not materials stuff. If you really wanna help me u will. U can use your charge card to buy them for me. But if u don't wanna do it, it is fine. I will still love you no matter what."

I wish he wouldn't keep saying that: "but I will still love you no matter what." That's what I crave, unconditional love. Don't we all?

I was running out of funds. I didn't have fifteen thousand dollars after withdrawing all I could from several smaller savings accounts, drawing from my retirement account, and even cashing in some twenty-year-old savings bonds. I did, however, have two charge cards with a $10k limit on each one. I had reservations about purchasing these expensive items and mailing them to Steve's buddy. Still, I shoved these thoughts to the back of my mind. I was determined to follow through with my commitment until the end, until Steve was back home. I worried that my children would find out. They knew I sent the computer to Selina for her birthday many months ago and weren't happy. When I got phone calls from "No Caller ID," they rolled their eyes but didn't say anything. I was always on edge around them. *They just don't understand how lonely I get. I want a partner by my side, especially as I get older. It's scary sometimes when an accident happens, or when I'm sick. Who's going to hold my hand?*

I sensed this was a crossroad, buying something and sending it to him. For one thing, I always paid the balance off each month and never carried a balance on my charge. I knew the interest rates were enormous, and purchasing these computers would put me in that situation. But, on the other hand, if I did come through and help him, I could make payments each month and live with a tighter budget. It would be possible. This was a more serious request, and I might get caught in several ways, which might end the relationship.

I wrote: "Steve, I don't have any more money to lend you. I think you'll go to jail, or maybe your anti-scam agents, Seth Jnr and Officer Martin can help you somehow. I'm preparing to leave on vacation next week. I'm about to cut you loose. You're causing me too much trouble."

I'll tell him that I can't help and see how he responds.

March 4, 2019, 1:25 p.m., Steve Cryer <Hangouts> "Honey, I will repay every penny you've spent to help me get my freedom. I'm so tired of this bullshit. I want to come home. I won't even bother you after I get home, and I'll repay you the money you've spent. Please help me. You are a kind person. I know you want to help me."

I'll sit here on the couch and try to decide what to do. What's going on with me? I should bring this to a halt. I know it's the logical move. I think I've spent about $75,000 on helping Steve, but I'm not in debt. It's comforting, a little. But, I'm pondering, how did I get to this point?

Can't even remember all the reasons for lending him this money. I just went through the motions, not thinking of what I was doing. Putting these purchases on my charge account is another situation entirely. I can't believe myself. Still, even with the stress of going into debt, I'm excited. I can do one more thing to help my soul mate return to me. I'm not at the end of options yet!

I wrote: "Steve, I'll purchase these six computers, putting them on my charge card, and then I'll be able to concentrate on my upcoming vacation. What do you think about that?"

March 4, 2019, 3:25 p.m., Steve Cryer <Hangouts> "Janet, you are my angel. I'm so grateful for your kindness and compassion. I could kiss you right now. Thank you for doing this one last favor."

Steve seemed calm and happy for the first in a long time since he arrived in New York City, almost two months ago. I was glad for him, but now my thoughts of finding stores that carried the computers, purchasing them, packaging, and mailing them were foremost in my mind. But I was determined not to let anything stop me. *When I make a decision, I stick to it.*

He advised I could purchase the computers and mail them through the United Parcel Service, UPS, to his friend, David Asante, who lived in Massachusetts. David would drive to the New York City airport with the boxes in his car to deliver them to Steve. Steve would secretly take them to the customs office before the boss returned from vacation. One customs officer advised if he replaced the computers, he wouldn't get into trouble. Otherwise, he would've been hauled off to jail that day. Even after replacing the computers, he still had to pay the shipping company bill of $20k before being free. Almost everyone treated Steve like a criminal, but there was always one person who was nice to him in every situation. This time it was one of the customs officers. I was grateful for that for him.

Even though the story of damaging those computers sounded so bizarre, I purposefully went to three different Best Buy stores to buy six of them. I was committed to helping Steve get his freedom, and I would stick by my word. It took two days to do this as there is a purchase limit of two computers unless it is for a business. I was surprised the stores didn't have their systems linked up. I would've thought they could see that I'd purchased computers at different locations, but they didn't question me.

The store clerks did ask what I was doing with these expensive, complex computers. I said I was giving them to my two grandchildren as graduation gifts. They were both in graphic art programs in college and needed machines capable of running complex software. Laughingly, I said the girls could figure out how to purchase the software themselves, as the computer was already a lovely gift. I was getting so good at telling a convincing story. It was as if I was writing a play and I was the actor. I would shiver in excitement when my story was successful.

One young clerk who waited on me said he wished I was his grandmother. He'd like a graduation gift like this. He was chatty, and that worked for me. This young man went on to tell me a story about himself. His grandmother had been a drug addict. His mother had planned to abort him and save her money for the procedure. But when she had to take grandma to the hospital, the abortion money went toward paying her bill. So, his mother didn't go through with the procedure, and he was born.

He's said, "I can't believe I told you that story. Hardly anyone knows that about me." I'd given this young man a chance to tell about himself and realize how fortunate he was today and every day of his life. It left me with such a warm charitable feeling, which lasted almost the whole day.

But, later that same day, David Asante in Massachusetts called Steve all upset, saying the mail lady came to his house and demanded back the package she'd delivered yesterday. *I mailed brown envelopes with $15,000 cash on February 28, and $18,000 on March 7th to David, Steve's new accomplice. I wonder if the Post Office found out there's cash in one of the envelopes?*

March 8, 2019, 1:25 p.m., Steve Cryer <Hangouts> "Janet, did you make a report to the US Post Office about David? He thought you might've been angry about having to purchase the computers and went ahead and took action about the envelope of cash."

I wrote: "Steve, my man, I have done no such thing, and I'm mailing six computers to David as we speak."

David isn't so sure I'd support Steve. Instead, he suspects I reported him to USPS. I didn't even consider making a report. For me, it's just better not to make waves, to keep doing what's easy. I avoid confrontation. I'm looking at the totals for the month of February and it's $57,000, and already in March it's been $25,000.

I wasn't involved with David's mail lady worry, but I thought about something else. I'd purchased their computers on my charge cards. The IP addresses were attached to my Best Buy account, including my home address and charge card information. Maybe someone would use the computers for illegal activity? Could I be held responsible if any of this happened? This possibility concerned me, but I said to myself, nothing terrible would ever happen to me. Finally, David called Steve back, saying the mail lady returned later that afternoon, apologizing for the error. She was confused, and the situation was for a different address.

March 9, 2019, 11:25 p.m., Steve Cryer <No caller ID> "Honey, after 11:00 p.m. this airport clears out and it gets quieter. No one will be using the bathroom, so I can have privacy and talk to you. How'd your day? I can't wait to be beside you in that king-sized bed, cuddling you and whispering in your ear. I will rub your back until you fall asleep."

I responded: "Steve, when I hear you say those lovely things, in your husky, sexy voice, I get all warm inside. We could be good together, you know? Don't mess this thing up."

March 10, 2019, 1:25 p.m., Steve Cryer <Hangouts> "I'm a little short here. All I need is $200. Can you help me? Once I get the computers replaced, I'll be free to go, and you're taking care of that for me. Martin received the money transfer from Seth Jnr, with the cash you mailed. So today he's in Accra paying the balance to the shipping company. I'm so close to being home with you."

I replied: "I took a photo of my MasterCard and texted it to you right now. You should be able to use it if necessary and buy some food to get you by. That card still has some credit available, even after purchasing the computers. I hate thinking you're hungry, as well as disappointed over the delay in getting home. I trust you." *I trust him only so far. From now on, I'll check my credit card balances more frequently. So far I haven't seen anything out of the ordinary.*

March 10, 2019, 1:55 p.m., Steve Cryer <Hangouts> "Honey, no I didn't use the card becos I'm not in the right sense now of eating or buying something. But I sat down and made a rough estimate and if we have $30,000 we can pay all the bills I still have. All along, I've been writing everything in a notebook."

I replied: "I'm glad you've been keeping track of what I've sent so that you can pay me back." My calculations of what I loaned him coincided with his, $117,000. But, what's he planning to tell or ask me about this $30K? I imagined there was a lot more in this notebook, too: names of my family and pets, when I had specific meetings each week, when I went to church, what day was grocery day, issues I had to deal with at my house, what car I drove, etc. He seemed to be up on all those details.

Steve claimed he'd protected me from scammers. He said he knew when I talked with another man on a dating site, which scared him. *How does he know I've been talking to another guy? Does he have access to my PoF account too?* He declared he wanted to keep me safe. I wondered if this was true? I chuckled under my breath. I think Steve wants to keep me all to himself!

14: THE TEAM

....

*"Always remember that you are absolutely unique.
Just like everyone else."*

—Margaret Mead

....

I was getting bored, tired of his excuses for not being able to come to me. When I didn't communicate with him as often as I'd been, he asked me what was wrong. I'd sent him a lot of cash and the computers, but then what? He still needed the $30,000 to allow him to get home. He maintained communication with me, but our evening chats were fewer and shorter in length, and they'd lost their intimacy. I suspected he was talking to several other women besides me. Could this be why he seemed more distant and not as attentive as earlier in the year?

Steve often told me all about the workings of scammers, maybe to impress me with his knowledge. He knew a lot about them, and I suspected some of his messages had been written by someone else, maybe even cut and pasted from an internet site that provided love messages. *Any resourceful guy would do his homework and search for sweet things to write to his girl!* Some messages were poorly written grammatically. Others didn't have many errors. He claimed his other friends would take care of money matters, including receiving the funds I sent, always within the states, and they transferred it to Steve, who was out of the country, or later in NYC. Steve seemed proficient on the computer and cell phone, and he changed his email account at least three times during our relationship and phone number several times. When he called me, "No Caller ID" would show up on my phone, so he knew how to hide his number. He had connections everywhere, as he was able to call Grandpa Allen in Missouri to get him to talk to me. He could send me a car. And yet, non of his friends helped him with money.

When we talked on the phone during the day in the early part of March, he was preoccupied. He was always getting calls from other people. He explained it was Seth Jnr or David Asante, or Officer Martin. He kept me on hold or told me he'd call me back. I was patient at first, but then I was annoyed and hung up. That phone was his way of communicating with his "team" and doing business, he explained. My heart raced every time I saw "No Caller ID" on my screen, and I thought my boyfriend was calling! *Am I that lonely and will drop everything just to talk to this guy for a few minutes?*

Steve convinced me he looked forward to being a family man. He talked about doing chores around the house, cooking for Selina and me, having a big powerful truck and another fancy vehicle. He said he'd set up a home for him and Selina with nice furniture and artwork. *I'm embarrassed to admit I'm influenced by wealth.* This father talked about putting his daughter in private school and was hopeful that I would help him do that. He claimed he wanted to set up investments with his money when he got home, to take care of his future. He praised me for taking care of my finances and hoped I would help him in that matter. *I'm flattered! But a wealthy person like he claimed he was wouldn't need any advice on investments, and I was indirectly revealing my income level. I shouldn't let my ego control my thoughts!*

I wondered if this man believed or intended to do anything he promised. I Googled his name and face and found other photos of him. One picture was of him with a nice-looking woman on his lap. She wore "Daisy Duke" shorts and had lovely long legs. I confronted him about it.

March 12, 2019, 1:25 p.m., Steve Cryer <Hangouts> "That was my daughter."

I replied: "I don't think so. You had your hand on her crotch."

March 12, 2019, 1:35 p.m., Steve Cryer <Hangouts> "I think you're a little jealous. That means you care about me. That's good. That was the poor waitress I told you about that I gave money to. We didn't date and I never even kissed her."

Did I mistrust this excuse? Yes. When I confronted him again, he admitted all the photos I'd found on the internet were not of him. He said they were of someone his team had copied from another's profile. Was he using this revelation about the fake photos as a way to convince me he could be honest? I didn't think to ask him for a "real" photo. Another crossroad, as I realized that a lot of his story is contrived, not just the photos. *What if I didn't have or didn't give him any money? Would he still be talking to me? I suspect the answer would be "no," but I can't deal with this now. I've invested money, time, and my heart. I can't face it. This can't be fake.*

It was becoming more evident that he wanted and even expected me to give up and quit sending money. I hadn't offered to help with this last $30k he said he needed, and he didn't ask for it. Now, his attempts to keep me engaged were few and far between.

March 13, 2019, 7:25 p.m., Steve Cryer <Hangouts> "Don't give up on me."

Like him, I didn't want him to give up on me! I was eager for this man to realize he needed me and forget about the money. I had so much love to give and was hungry to share it. I'd stick by him through the good and bad times if he would come home and commit to me. My heart ached, and I felt like it would burst. I was lonely and longed to experience the plans we'd made together.

Steve often called me on Sunday afternoons, after I came home from Mass. I told him I had prayed for him and Selina and hoped he'd be able to return home soon. Sundays were one of the loneliest days of the week. I longed to have my man beside me in the church pew, with our shoulders touching sensitively as we quietly prayed together. I craved his touch, and I knew he would be sensitive, by his voice. I'd spent ten intense months nourishing this relationship and was ready for the harvest.

15: FEET TO THE FIRE

Middle March 2019

....

*"Never let the fear of striking out
keep you from playing the game."*

—Babe Ruth

....

"Steve, I think it is important for me to see you now, in order to continue my faith in this relationship. I don't get the same feeling from you."

March 12, 2019, 1:25 p.m., Steve Cryer <Hangouts> "I'm ready for u. What do you mean by u don't get the same feelings from me? If I don't want this to work why will I still be here trying to make this work and watching out for you. I'm ready to meet u and see u but never blame me when your caught and we are to pay more money. I'm ready to die with u and ready to do anything to make u happy. So come to me if that is what u wanna risk. I love u and miss u."

I replied: "Okay. I can add a day before my North Carolina trip and come to NYC. I'm sure I can be reasonably safe if I get off the plane and go directly to a hotel. Then you try to meet me there, okay?"

March 12, 2019, 1:45 p.m., Steve Cryer <Hangouts> "Yes, but I need to settle payment before I leave due to the fact that this laptop issues is messing me up. Once I pay and solve it I can meet u at the airport hotel u will be in."

I wrote: "Well, the laptop issue can't be solved till your agent brings the ones I sent him, and the earliest that would be is Friday. So, I guess you can't leave the airport?" I was comforted when Steve spoke of trying to keep me safe, safe from the officials who would do anything to get my money, and that he even considered meeting me. I was so hungry for his sweet voice, gentle touch, and handsome face.

March 12, 2019, 1:55 p.m., Steve Cryer <Hangouts> "Yes, I can only leave once David brings the laptops here."

I wrote: "This's very complicated. I'll let you know what I decide."

March 12, 2019, 1:58 p.m., Steve Cryer <Hangouts> "I'm a pain in the butt, forgive me."

***

I was preparing to leave for a six-day visit to my daughter's family on the East coast. I took care of all my commitments to Steve to facilitate his release from bondage (sending cash, buying, and sending six computers). I told him I was totally out of cash, and my charge cards were almost to the maximum after I'd purchased the computers. *I'm not sure I'll be able to pay for my gas to get to and from the airport or pay for parking there.* I'd never had my charge cards to an amount I couldn't pay at the end of the month. I was more nervous than ever about my finances. It's one thing to spend frivolously, but another to go into debt. I was nervous about being with the family and careful not to let much slip out about this relationship. I'll have to act like a happy grandma and play with the grandchildren. *I'm so tired of keeping this a secret.*

My daughter and kids picked me up at the airport with their new puppy, and it was a joyous reunion. I was relieved to have this diversion. I secretively texted Steve and his daughter Selina while I was away. I tried desperately to keep up with conversations at my daughter's home and appear to be normal.

Even while on vacation, I checked my emails to and from Officer Martin. I learned my money had gotten to him to pay the shipping costs, but unfortunately, he said, they took a lot of handling fees out of it. He didn't have enough to pay the $20k. And guess what, there was an additional $12,000 insurance on the gold storage. *All that work to scrape up money for the last bills, and it's not enough! I'm going to cry. Better hold it together for the kids' sake.*

I was scared my relationship with Steve would end because I had run out of money. I was afraid my family would put all their observations together and somehow stop me. Could this tender-sounding man be deceiving me? Was it possible he didn't care about me at all, that he never intended to come home to be with me? But when I heard his voice, all doubts were forgotten. I desperately wanted his words to be valid.

March 17, 2019, 1:25 p.m., Steve Cryer <Hangouts> "I will never lie to you Janet. Trust me. Don't give up on me. And, I still need about $30k before I'll be free."

I wrote: "Steve, my children have been watching my cats while I'm gone. I suspect they are looking around my house, and snooping through the papers on my desk and trying to access my computer. They know where to find my passwords. I'm concerned they will find bank receipts and the addresses of Seth Jnr and David Asante."

One day in the middle of my visit, I received a text message from my daughter Susan back home. She asked whose blue Toyota was parked in my driveway. I said, "A friend's. I'm letting him park it there for a few days." She said, "A local friend?" I said, "Sure." She didn't believe me, I could tell, but she didn't push it.

I arrived home from my visit on a Tuesday afternoon. I took all that day and Wednesday to catch up on sleep and recover from the traveling. I wonder if the children at home had talked about the Toyota? My daughter Susan worked for the local sheriff's department and researched these things. I knew she'd dig into this.

Even after I arrived home, Steve asked about my cats and how I was feeling, but nothing was said about the kids' questions about the car in my driveway. Mostly, he was lamenting about the new development, the insurance company needed money.

Thursday, March 21, I woke up that morning after a fretful sleep. I ventured into the family room and began my prayer routine. I prayed for guidance and strength, for the faith to accept "Thy Will Be Done." I unconsciously paged through a magazine, not seeing the words at all. There was a heaviness in my body. I was very tired of my life and feared rejection by this man I thought I loved. I felt like I was a part of the couch. My body felt heavy, and my neck could hardly support my head. I had a dreadful feeling. I sensed the kids were communicating about the Toyota car and maybe something they found in the house while I was gone on my visit out east.

March 21, 2019, 1:25 p.m., Steve Cryer <Hangouts> "How're you?"

I texted: "Not so good. And don't call me either because I don't want you to hear my tearful voice." *My prayers are not taking away the tears. I'm so exhausted.*

March 21, 2019, 1:30 p.m., Steve Cryer <Hangouts> "plz honey, talk to me." When I didn't respond to this text he called me.

March 21, 2019, 1:40 p.m., Steve Cryer <No caller ID> "Please don't give up on me."

I reluctantly answered, but I didn't say much as I was crying so uncontrollably. Steve did all the talking and was acting differently. His voice was clear and deliberate, and I sensed this might be his last-ditch effort to appeal to me.

He continued: "How're you doing and why trying to be distant again whiles I always try to work things out? Last night I dreamed Ray (my late husband) came to me and asked me to take care of you, because he was taken early and wouldn't be able to do it. 'Take care of her like a queen,' he said. 'She's taken care of everything by herself and now needs to be taken care of.' Please, Janet, don't give up on me."

Without responding, I slid my thumb over the red hang-up button on my phone, and pressed it down. I put my hands to my stomach and pulled my knees up to my chest. I sat there on the couch shuddering, like it was suddenly cold in the room, and pressed my fist against my mouth to suppress any sound from coming out. Even though I was alone in the house, I stayed silent. I was afraid to break the spell and feared what would come next.

16: THE INTERVENTION

*"To live is to experience pain, but to survive
is to find meaning and purpose in the pain."*

—*Viktor Frankl*

The afternoon of Thursday, March 21, 2019, I looked up from the couch in my family room, where I hadn't moved since the emotional morning phone call with Steve. I saw and heard several cars drive up. I noticed my son and three daughters emerge from those vehicles, and then I knew they'd come to confront me. My heart started racing. I was getting defensive by the minute, as I knew this was my children coming to me with concerns, and I feared all my secrets about the last ten months would come out.

My initial reaction was anger at my children for descending upon my home, and I asked them, "What the hell are you all doing here?" This group included my daughter Sam, from out east, who I'd left two days ago. I knew this visit wouldn't be good if she flew all this way so soon. *Did they plan to gang up on me?*

I heard someone question, "Where do we sit?"

I blurted, "In the family room I guess, as this looks like a family gathering." Tears started cascading down my cheeks, and sweat beaded up on my forehead and other parts of my body. I was shivering, staring down at my hands as we all sat down. I ignored their facial expressions of fear, anger, concern.

Each of them held a paper within their hands, letters they had prepared to disclose their feelings, I assume, written down so they wouldn't forget what they wanted to say.

I sat numbly, not sure I wanted to hear any of it, yet I had no choice.

They said, "We're here because you're our Mom and we love you." "You deserve to be happy." "When you started online dating, you set some reasonable boundaries for yourself, but since that time you've changed so much in your behavior." "We fear for your safety, and that of the whole family." "You are a victim of online fraud." "This is not you!" "We can't imagine the stress you're going through." "Ninety percent of the time you would smell a snake out like this, as thrifty as we were raised." "We know this isn't something you would do." "Something is very wrong with you right now," "Please understand things in life happen and now is the time to take action and end this." "Let us help you."

I silently cried while they spoke, listening to the sincerity and concern in their voices. I questioned my sanity! *How did all of this happen? What made me do it?* It's evident to them how I had become a victim. Why couldn't I see it? They seemed surprised and relieved when I agreed to accept their assistance in trying to recover from things I'd done. *Recover? I'll never be the same as before this experience, but do I even want to be?* We all knew there was little hope of recovering any money.

My daughter, Marie, the one I attend Mass with every Sunday and have coffee chats with afterward, was absent from the meeting. The others had given her a later arrival time for the discussion. While doing the research, the other four had discovered many of my illogical behaviors and actions, and they suspected I'd included Marie in some of my secrets during our coffee chats. They were concerned she might be offended by their intervention and would protect my privacy.

Marie cautiously slipped into the family room. Someone briefed her on what they had done, and I noticed her body slump a bit before she took her place in the room. She sat next to me on the couch, and when the others detailed their reason for the meeting, I could feel the tenseness leave her body. Then, she gave me a huge hug. I now realize it was a significant burden on her to have known about Steve. Never about the money. But I shared the heartaches from not being able to meet him. I felt guilt and remorse for putting her in that position. I hoped our special relationship wasn't ruined.

After the session with my children, I invited my friend Mary Ann, my brother and sister-in-law, and my cousin to the house. While my children surrounded me, I wanted to come clean with them, too, regarding my personal ten-month dating journey. They'd probably noticed some different behaviors in me too, and I needed to explain. They sat in my living room, not making a sound, listening to my explanation. Mary Ann sat forward on the couch, motionless, intently listening to my every word. Later, she said it felt like I was sharing the news of a family member's death. She said I was so somber and ashen in color as I spoke.

I told them my story, but it felt like I wasn't even there in the room. It was someone else talking, not me. I shared the frustration and anger for not controlling my actions, even when I suspected I was being deceived. I was relieved to have it all out in the open, even if there were many more details I hadn't yet shared.

My daughter Susan contacted the police, and an officer came out to the house that afternoon. He sat uncomfortably on the couch in the living room and said: "Tell me what happened."

For the next thirty minutes, I peered directly into the eyes of this policeman I'd never met. It was quite a different sensation. Usually, I would begin to sweat in the presence of an officer of the law. Instead, I had his undivided attention and was getting a kick out of it. This was enjoyable! I told the story, mainly including the part about the Toyota. He said he couldn't do much about my dilemma except he could have the car hauled away and investigate it. I didn't see him write one thing in the little notebook he held tightly in his hands, even though he had it posed with the pencil ready to record something. He didn't ask for any addresses or phone numbers of Steve Cryer, nor any of the other people I had communicated with. Finally, he wrote my phone number down. He had to write something! Susan ushered him out and chatted with him before he made his way back to his office. That was all there was to it. She later learned that the car was stolen and the title was fake. There was an official police report generated from the meeting, but the officer said there was little the police could do to retrieve any money. I had willingly given the money.

By the end of the day, I was exhausted, and maybe in shock too. A lot had happened in eight hours. That evening, I slid under the covers in my king-sized bed alone. I had made serious mistakes. *Had I been foolish to think love could happen?* I knew my life would change drastically from this moment on, and the battle would be greater than the last ten months of keeping secrets. Even though I'd never met Steve, I still believed I knew him. His handsome face was seared into my memory (at least the face in the photos), and his deep voice was still in my brain, although it was slowly fading. I fought this loss, as I had fought to retain the memory of my youngest son's voice some years before. Would I recover and learn to be contented? The answer to that question was uncertain. Even though I'd had a wonderful life, certainly it'd now be different than I'd ever known. I was desperate to get beyond this stage, but change takes time. I knew I couldn't sleep it off like a hangover. This would take work!

After the family meeting was over and the policeman and extended family left, I felt the need to hibernate. I couldn't bear to go out into the community and face people. I thought everyone would learn about my idiotic decisions and judge me. News like this travels at lightning speed in small towns like mine. I believed my wonderful reputation was frayed, like worn blue jeans. So far, the few people I'd come in contact with just stared at me. I saw in their eyes a shocked look, and I imagined them saying to themselves, "Holy Shit, Janet, how could you have done all that?"

I had lost over $100k to this man. It was my travel money and a rainy day fund. My husband's retirement, some savings, and social security benefits would enable me to live comfortably for the rest of my years. It was a relief to know this, and I was very grateful.

17: REBUILDING

"If you're brave enough to say goodbye,
life will reward you with a new hello."

—unknown author

I didn't know if I could write this book and share it with anyone else. The shame is so embedded in my heart. I know other women have succumbed to doing as I have. Some have gotten even deeper into the fraud scheme and lost more money than I had, but that doesn't make me feel better. It's something I'll always carry with me, like a cross I must bear. Join the human race, right?!

My children assisted and encouraged me to delete the phone numbers and emails from Steve Cryer, his daughter, Selina, and his friend, Officer Martin. My children each have a different area of "expertise," and they quickly got to work. My daughter Lynn is a financial officer in the government, so she began changing logins and passwords on my bank accounts, Facebook account, changed my cell phone number, and put privacy locks on it. She signed me up for

LifeLock, a service that tracks fraudulent activity for individuals. Finally, she initiated an investigation with the U.S. Treasury Department.

My daughter Susan made reports to the local police and FBI, initiating a report on the "Internet Crime Complaint Center – IC3" and investigated transactions in my bank accounts. She was a co-signer on one bank account, but I guess she had never looked into it. Over the last months, I worried she would do that, and my secret would be out. That weighed heavily on my mind every day.

My daughter Sam called around and arranged for an intake that day with a therapist and made me an appointment for the next week to start individual counseling. The three girls went with me to the counselor's office. Sitting there in the crowded waiting area, I felt like a bad kid. I hid my face and slumped down in the soft leather chair. During the intake, the therapist asked me to describe the reason for my visit. I started to tell her about my dating experience, but my daughter interjected a few additional details. She told the woman I had lost my youngest son in Afghanistan, that my middle son attempted suicide, and was diagnosed with schizophrenia, and my husband died suddenly five years before. The woman stared at her keyboard and patiently typed this information into her computer. *I wonder what she thinks about all this? Is she in shock, or is it what she hears every day? Sure would like to know what's she typing on the form. Am I crazy?*

The girls went with me to the bank and credit union the next day, where we canceled all my accounts and opened new ones. We opened a post office box and started forwarding my mail to that address. The police officer had listened to my story and made arrangements to remove the car. He made a call, and the vehicle was gone.

My son Kevin was concerned for my safety and wanted to protect me. He wanted me to leave the house for a while. The fact that Steve knew my address bothered him a lot. I told him I wasn't scared, primarily embarrassed.

After Thursday, March 21, 2019, I began a long "rebuilding" period, as my therapist calls it. I met with her every week at first. Those visits were small comfort to me, a safe place to unload, and occurred in the neighboring town. I was so embarrassed for the first few weeks and didn't want to be seen anywhere in my town. I knew I'd break down and cry at the minor little thing and would make a spectacle of myself. I was so nervous talking to the clerk about renting a post office box at the post office. *Just a week before, I mailed over $10,000 in a plain brown envelope, and I wasn't nearly as nervous then as I am now! My emotions were on my face. I wanted to run away, far, far away.*

My experience was more complicated than losing money and being embarrassed. It was the emotional loss. I was heartbroken. I felt abandoned, rejected. I'd unknowingly allowed Steve to steer me in the direction he wanted, and during that time, I fell in love. He convinced me that if I cared for him and wanted him by my side, I'd do what he asked. His sweet, patient voice was a "drug" that I'd become addicted to. I did have a sneaking suspicion some of his promises were lame, and I couldn't fully trust him. But I wanted this so badly I ignored my innermost thoughts.

When reading in my devotional prayerbooks, I heard Steve's voice in my head saying the Lord's words. "Call me gently to arouse my love…." I couldn't get his voice or the image of his face out of my mind. I was in love with the man behind the screen. Even though he wasn't the man in the photos, I still had feelings for him. It was the person, not the face, that made me feel wanted and less alone. Even with all the heartache and pain I was going through now, I had a deep fondness for him.

Now, so many things would trigger an internal panic attack. Driving by one of those banks I had gone to for Steve would make me cry. I've not been able to shop at a Best Buy store yet, and I'm not too fond of post offices. I've relived those awful moments over and over. Looking at a crisp new $100 bill or a brown envelope triggers an anxious moment too. Will I ever be able to act normally in these situations? I'm told, one way is to push through the situation, and that, eventually, my brain will allow me to get through it without the panicky feeling.

So, the rebuilding that I needed to do involved learning that I would be okay. I'll find meaning and purpose again. I hope that It'll be better than before, because if my life was okay then, why did I think I needed someone to fill in the gaps and make my life complete? Maybe when I am more content with myself, I will allow others to appreciate and enjoy my company.

I knew this wouldn't be easy, but I surrounded myself with a support network. Next, I must learn to take advantage of the offers of help if they're helpful and reject those that aren't. Finally, I must learn to say NO, and explaining isn't necessary. This is a damn slow process. BABY STEPS, BABY!

***

Steve called a couple of days after "The Intervention." I was pretty sure it was him calling when the number showed up "No Caller ID" on my home landline. I'd never given him this number. I wasn't sure what I'd do when and if this happened, so, even though I'd told my children I wouldn't talk to him again, I couldn't resist. I picked it up.

I said, "Hello."

He said: "HI."

I asked, even though I knew, "Who is this?"

He said: "Honey, don't you know who this is?"

I hung up. It was exhilarating to hear Steve's voice and exciting to think he might still want to talk to me. But, I had promised my children I wouldn't talk to him, so I didn't continue the conversation. *Damn, this is so hard to do. Maybe he still wants me?* I sat there on my kitchen stool, immobile for a few minutes. I couldn't help myself but kept repeating his voice in my head. I loved hearing his voice!

The thirty-second interaction interrupted my attempt to purge Steve Cryer from my life. In my mind, I wanted to be free from him, but my heart resisted. He didn't abandon me. I broke it off with him. Yet, I still pined for his affection, the man that made me feel young, attractive, and desired. For a time, he had eased my loneliness.

I routinely checked my email accounts for messages I might need to answer the following week. I noticed an unusual one on the new account Lynn had set up for me. I'd only given this information to my five children, so I hardly ever got a message here. But there was one from Officer Martin. How did he get this address?

From: Martin Willson<martinjob1947@gmail.com
Date: Tuesday, March 26, 2019
Subject: About your Husband, he is Admitted and is
Urgent
To: Janet Marshall

Dear Madam. May I know why you changed your phone number? I ask because this all part of why he went on to do this stupid act, even if you don't love him, don't stop communicating with him. Please talk to him till he heals, and maybe you can decide to keep him or not. He don't need this at this time.

From: Janet Marshall
To: Martin Willson <martinjob1947@gmail.com
Date: Tuesday, March 26, 2019

Martin,

I'm so sorry to hear this. I, too, have been ill and under a doctor's care with medication and therapy. I hope he gets the help he needs. Janet

I knew Martin, whoever he was, was fabricating this lie. They had to try to get me back in the game one more time. I wanted them to know I was in pain and that finally, I was giving up. Maybe they would give up too. I hoped so.

18: RIDING THE FENCE

One night, several months after I'd broken it off with Steve, I was absentmindedly watching an insignificant movie on TV. From across the room, I heard a male voice. My heart skipped a beat, and then I focused my attention on the television screen. This actor spoke with the same speech and accent as Steve Cryer had. I hadn't talked to him in a while, but I still remembered that voice so well. *Steve never left me a voice message, nor was I able to record his voice, so it's just in my memory. I think he deliberately avoided recording his voice.* The actor in this movie was supposed to be from Germany or Poland. Was Steve possibly German, like he said? Steve claimed he would never lie to me. Was that the truth? I'm going to turn the TV off and sit here in silence, searing that voice in my head, so I can enjoy the exhilarating feeling for as long as It'll last.

Hearing a similar voice on the TV is one example of how hard it is to purge your mind of a manipulative relationship, to restore normalcy after being duped. Little things come up now and then with no warning.

Even though I now know it was all a scam, I still have moments to question things. It's so easy to go right back into reviving the mindset: the man loved me, and wanted to be with me. It's like an impulse I can't control. My mind would start racing, thinking back about all the conversations. Like the actor's accent on the TV, any new observation brings it back again. This brief experience made me realize I still hadn't gotten over the mystery man.

I continued to carry my cell phone everywhere and even put it near my head as I slept. I obsessively checked it every few minutes to see if I had a missed call or message. Then, in the middle of the night, I'd awaken and check it too. I had now blocked all the contacts for Steve and his friends, but he could probably find me. The call would show "No Caller ID" on my screen if he did. I told myself I wouldn't answer if that happened, but I still desired to know if he'd attempted to get in touch. That'd be so satisfying. He'd learned my new number once before, without me telling him, so I hoped he would go to that effort again. Then I would know he cared for me, not just my money or what I could do for him.

This obsession hindered my "recovery," so my therapist suggested I put the phone someplace far away for even a few hours every night to give me some peace. I put it in the garage, and I wouldn't touch it most nights. But occasionally, I felt the need to talk to someone, actually Steve, so I retrieved the phone and put it beside my bed again. *Maybe he'll try to call me, and I'll feel better for a while?* When in the grip of grief, everything and everyone is a reminder of the loss. Like driving past the post offices where I mailed the cash, or the Best Buy stores where I bought the computers, or the stores where I bought the brown envelopes. It took several months before I could occasionally think about other things and not hope for contact from Steve.

I imagined what I'd do if Steve knocked on my door one day. I knew I wouldn't turn him away. After I heard his voice, even if I didn't recognize his face, I'd quickly hug him and hold on tight. I know I would. I wasn't over this!

I pray that scammers on the internet feel horrible about the pain their actions cause and that they'll quit the business. Maybe they could parlay their talents to act in movies and be legitimate employees of a thriving industry. Films need to be written and produced with stories like mine so that women can learn from them and not fall prey to the "lions" prowling the online dating world.

I am very grateful that I never committed any illegal act. I didn't take out loans (except for using my charge cards), mortgage my home, or sell possessions. I now need to budget my spending, but I'm fortunate to be able to still live comfortably.

***

My girlfriend stopped for a visit one Friday morning. I think it was in the month of May. While she and I were having coffee in the dining room, someone knocked on the front door. *Who could this be? I'm not expecting anyone.* But, instead, a short, middle-aged dark-skinned man stood on the porch.

"I'm here to pick up a blue Toyota car," the man said with a little bit of an accent.

I looked at the logo on his shirt and the car hauler in my driveway. I noticed the company wasn't local, but was from Detroit. I walked outside, and my girlfriend followed me.

"I don't have the car anymore. I had it towed away. Look around if you need to." I motioned with my arms, indicating he was free to search my property for the vehicle. *It's been six weeks since I've heard from Steve. Does he never give up?*

As he backed away, the man handed me his phone. "The guy wants to talk to you."

Excitedly, I put it to my ear. "Hello, who's this?" *I hope it's him. I remember how his voice made me feel so happy.*

"You know. Why did you change your cell phone number?" It was Steve's normal voice, the relaxed tone he often used. But, I was stunned by the unexpected visit. I didn't know what to say.

I said: "The car isn't here, and where are you? That little blue car was for your errands when you got back to Michigan, you said." I knew he would lie to me, but I was flabbergasted he would go to this effort to try to reach me, six weeks after I had stopped all communications with him.

Steve said: "Calm down, calm down." A little louder this time, but still not angry. "Where is the car?"

I said: "You didn't answer my question. Where are you?" If I couldn't think of anything profound to say, at least I could demonstrate my feelings with an aggravated tone of voice.

After a slight hesitation, he said: "New York." I detected a southern drawl—Nu Yolk. *Where did that accent come from? Was he from Missouri?*

I immediately replied, "Bull crap, you're not in New York, and it's true, the car isn't here. I had it hauled away." I ended the call, not wanting to hear another word from his lying mouth, and handed the phone back to the truck driver. He came near enough to me to accept it with an outstretched hand. It seemed he didn't want to get close to me at all. *I had intimidated him. Good.* He looked like he wished he hadn't been assigned a job with this irate woman, me.

I told the driver, "This guy is a very bad man, and he hurt me. You shouldn't ever do business with him again." I couldn't believe what had come from my mouth, a fourth-grade tirade from a child affronted on the playground! But, if I couldn't come up with the words I wanted, at least I demonstrated the emotion behind the statement, and it was effective with this stranger. Even before he left my front porch, I heard him back on his phone reporting to his boss word for word what I'd said.

I could've told Steve the police had the damn car. I could've asked him how he felt after supposedly being in the hospital under the surgeons' knife and almost dying. I could've told him I canceled my bank account, and the numbers he said he knew didn't exist any longer. I could've told him he could repay all the thousands I lent him by sending a check to my address, as he obviously knew it. But I didn't say anything of the sort. I was too stunned.

Steve called back again right away. Even at the far end of my driveway, I heard the driver answer his phone and immediately blurt out, "The lady doesn't want to talk to you, and I can't force her to speak to you. There is no car here, and I've looked all around the house." The driver got back in his truck and drove away.

I was shaken up, torn between being fearful of what could've happened and being elated by rekindling memories of hearing his voice. *But, Steve was helpless to force me to do anything now!* During this brief interaction, my heart rate was going through the roof. My hands were shaking but clutched together in an attempt to steady them. Luckily, I was not alone that day. Otherwise, if I had been alone, I may have acted differently. *I don't know. Maybe I would've called 911? Probably not. But, I felt powerful standing up to him.*

I wasn't angry that Steve had called. Even after these six weeks, his voice hypnotized me into wanting him again. I wished I hadn't talked to him so harshly. I loved hearing his little chuckles and his "calm down, calm down" to keep me on the phone line. He deserved my outrage, but still, I ached inside to hear him tell me he missed me, that he couldn't get me out of his mind, and plead with me to give him another chance. And he knew it! I saw many calls from Steve on my cell phone over the next few weeks, sometimes ten or more in a row. I never picked up, though. I compare this feeling to what a recovering alcoholic might experience when he sees or smells liquor. Even though we commit to abstaining from our drug of choice, it's so easy to lose control. But, I had a promise to keep to my children, and my girlfriend was there that day for support.

***

In this story, I should include a list of all the money I sent to Steve Cryer over the ten months I corresponded with him. I kept accurate records of the money transferred or mailed, and the amount I spent on the computers. Unfortunately, now that I see those records, I can't recall and haven't recorded the purpose for each of them. But the receipts and bank statements don't lie. I was out a total of $121,000. I probably won't ever recover these funds, but I can still live a comfortable life, unlike some women and even men, who sent their last dime to a scammer. By the grace of God, I've been spared this outcome.

Date	Dollars	Purpose/Method
2018.7.10	402	Selina's computer
2018.8.23	5,000	Transfer to Seth
2018.8.21	3,000	Transfer to Seth
2018.9.6	300	Transfer to Seth
2018.11.13	8,500	Transfer to Seth
2018.12.18	8,000	Transfer to Patricia D.
2019.1.5	6,000	Transfer to Patricia D.
2019.1.9	1,100	Mailed cash to Seth
2019.1.10	3,800	Mailed cash to Seth
2019.2.4	6,000	Mailed cash to Seth
2019.2.20	12,000	Mailed cash to Seth
2019.2.27	14,000	Mailed cash to Seth
2019.2.28	15,000	Mailed cash to Seth
2019.3.7	18,000	Mailed cash to Seth
2019.3.13	7,000	Mailed cash to Seth
2019.3.12	13,000	Computers
TOTAL	121,102	

19: MY RENAISSANCE

As I stated early on in my story, I bet most people who know me would say, "No, not Janet. She'd never do such things." *I can hardly believe it myself.* This is one reason why it is so important to record my experience. I hope people who read this realize anyone can get caught in a scammer's spider web of lies. These people know how to deceive and convince others to trust them.

I ask myself, who do I want to be now? I'm beginning to understand some of the motivations for my actions. First, I was lonely, bored, and looking for adventure. Through the months of talking to Steve, I'd changed my objective and determined I wanted a partner to share my life with. And too, if I hadn't gotten some satisfaction from the interactions with Steve, I wouldn't have pressed on through the frustrating times. This modest satisfaction led to addiction. I was compelled to do whatever Steve asked of me, just to hear his compliments and promises of his love and protection. Realistically, I'll probably make many more mistakes in my life, but I've learned some red flags to look for, and I hope I won't be blind to fake attention ever again.

I'm grateful for my children. I put them through embarrassment, caused them to mistrust me, and jeopardized our family's safety. So, I thank them for bravely intervening in my life to save me from financial ruin and emotional collapse. Once the details of my story are known, I anticipate family, friends, and acquaintances will question my actions. Still, I trust they'll forgive me in time.

Keeping secrets was not easy. It has taken a lot of concentration and strength to build a cover story and stick with it. I was a fraud in that sense. The deception eroded my self-confidence and affected my personality. Before this experience, I was a cheerful, confident woman, at least on the exterior. After ten months of brainwashing and manipulation by Steve, I was suspicious of people, uncomfortable in groups, super conscious of being alone. I hate sitting in church all alone, going to a restaurant alone, and am conscious of everyone sitting in pairs. I'd given up on myself. I thought the real Janet wasn't good enough to deserve a respectable man. During those ten months, I fantasized about being someone else and was acting that scenario out.

I own my mistakes. No one made me carry through with any of these regretful deeds. I settled for those men that gave me attention and ignored the value in myself. I needed to be needed, and the scammers honed in on that. Steve, and a couple of other men I happened to attract for a short time, also scammers, used the words "you are my savior, my angel, my queen." The text messages were temporary rewards. I imagined things would be different one day, that Steve would actually come home and be with me permanently.

I'd put my children first for so many years. It was my excuse for not caring for myself, both physically and emotionally. How could I manage a family of nine, dealing with an often-absent husband, who seemed to work too much? There was no time! Well, I thought so then. Later, I didn't want to admit how much satisfaction I got from my teaching career and sometimes put more effort into school than my own family. Nevertheless, I trust our home life provided some beneficial lessons for the kids, as they have all become responsible, resilient adults. And I hope they know I love them unconditionally.

I'm now motivated to make adjustments to my life. Firstly, my living situation needed to be changed. I'd lived alone for five years and managed to take care of the duties of a forty-year-old home. I hired people to do the things my husband had always done. After becoming widowed, my friends and family hinted that I should sell the house and move into something smaller with less upkeep. I was stubborn. Even then, I didn't like people telling me what I should do, except for the conman Steve Cryer.

When the scammers learned of my address and sent two strange men to my house, the car delivery man, and the car pick-up man, I decided my children were right. I wasn't safe there anymore. I use the plural form, "scammers," as Steve Cryer was not alone. I'm convinced he worked with a team of experienced manipulators. So why would I keep this huge home? So my children would have their childhood home? Maybe a good reason, but alone I couldn't take care of the place much longer.

I put the home up for sale on June 15, 2019, and sold it in five days. But, I had forty years of household stuff to sort through, so there were many obstacles in completing this move. But I'd made the decision, and now it was just carrying through with it. I could write a "what to do and what not to do" story about that monumental project. I loved my flower gardens. Over the years, I'd accumulated a multitude of perennials in brilliant colors blooming throughout the spring, summer, and fall. Unfortunately, I couldn't bring any outside flowers with me to a condominium, but my children dug up a lot and replanted them at their homes. So, I can still visit the kids and the flowers!

Then, I bought a condominium and moved in two months later. It was located in a fifty-five-and-up community with abundant activities and new people to meet. This change was the beginning of a whole new chapter of my life, "My Renaissance"— and as Shakespeare said, "fear not the shadows." Luckily it was summer, so many people were out and about in the community. Everyone waved at passers-by in this new neighborhood, so I was sure I'd be able to make new friends.

Finally, I continued to meet with my therapist bi-monthly. I found it helpful to bounce ideas off her, and she has become someone I trust. She listened to my problems, like my obsession with looking at my phone, hoping to see a message from Steve. As months pass by, I've resigned myself to the fact that he wasn't a real boyfriend. It was an illusion, so the only thing I'm grieving are the thoughts I had about someone who didn't exist. It'll take some time, but it's cathartic to put these memories to paper. I think of it as peeling an onion, one layer at a time. I don't want to be afraid any longer that time has passed me by or I won't be able to attract a good man. I am content in my new home and welcome fresh opportunities.

If my experience can help even one woman who might believe a con artist loves her, then I will have restitution. It's been quite a fiasco, and I don't want even one more person to fall into the trap and experience the pain associated with the emotional and financial losses. I pray I'll be able to trust, respect, and yield my heart to a partner one day. And I long for forgiveness, from God, my family, friends, and myself. I'm optimistic my story can be a model of resilience for those who undergo their own difficulties.

So, who do I want to be now? I want to be a better version of myself. I'm willing to get back up on the horse and try dating again. I appreciate this experience as a whole. It's forced me to look at myself in a different light and make changes, ones that I wouldn't have accomplished without this impetus. The emotional scars are there, but I'm hopeful. The more I learn about myself, the more I realize how complex human beings are. Knowledge is the introduction to healing. Then comes the lifework of developing new skills and attitudes to become the best version of oneself.

"It always seems impossible until it's done."

—*Nelson Mandela*

20: HOW CAN I HELP OTHERS?

RED FLAGS TO LOOK FOR—HOW TO SPOT A SCAM

Likely targets: We're probably very trusting people, but we might not fully grasp the extent some people will go to lie and deceive. We're probably the type who's compassionate toward someone who says they're in need too. And if we're honest, we're a little lonely, but that doesn't mean we're desperate. I've compiled a list of "red flags" that might indicate a fake suitor, especially when entering the world of online dating. In addition, I suggest you do an image search of pictures they send or post.

Any of the following may occur.

1. In emails, phone chats, and texting, he calls you: baby, babe, my love, my queen, darling, honey, hun, sweetie, etc., right away in the 1st or 2nd contact.

2. A scammer replies to your emails very quickly, within minutes, and has hours to chat with you at all hours of the day and night.

3. A scammer comes up with reasons why he can't meet you in person, and he never will.

4. A scammer declares he is new to the dating site, maybe new to online dating. He states he wants a long-term relationship.

5. Facts are inconsistent, i.e., age, birthday, height, where he is from. He may have two first names as his full name. Ie. James William.

6. A scammer will quickly send you sugar-coated and heart-winning love emails, rather than "Hi, how are you. I'd like to get to know you?"

7. A scammer usually has no family, business associates, or close friends, so he only has you to turn to.

8. A scammer may claim he's widowed or divorced and probably has a long sad story. He quickly states, "I love you," and has a grandiose story.

9. A scammer proclaims within a short time, "It was destiny or fate that we found each other."

10. A scammer gives only attractive details about himself. He can do anything, and do it well.

11. Scammers often don't capitalize "I," the cities and states' names, and misspell them.

12. He asks if you are chatting with other men. He wants you off the dating site so other scammers can't get to you. But, he doesn't want any competition from "real" men either.

13. A scammer refers to God and may even quote Bible scriptures to gain your trust. He claims to have a strong faith in God. He may even want to pray with you.

14. A scammer's occupation might be engineering, construction, oil drilling, geology, business, or one requiring travel. He won't tell you he's a doctor, teacher, factory worker, or another stable profession.

15. A scammer might ask for more photos of you and give you lots of compliments. He tells you his webcam or camera on his cell phone doesn't work, so he can't make live video chats. It's a lie! He might send several photos of himself (stolen from other men's profiles), often illustrating his job, his vehicles, and places where he's traveled.

16. A scammer probably has poor spelling and grammar. He might say he's educated, but apparently, he didn't learn to spell. Some say if you overlook these errors, you'll probably be a good mark, so that the errors could be intentional.

17. A scammer might refer to the United States as the USA and doesn't know much about the US, even though he knows about current world events as he watches CNN every morning.

18. Common themes for scammers to get money from you: travel, illness, investment failures, banking delays, illness of child or parent, or an accident. He says he needs money to pay customs charges, purchase equipment, pay his employees, or start a job.

19. A scammer promises any money you lend him, he'll pay back with interest.

20. A scammer asks you to wire money through a bank, credit union, Western Union, or Money Gram. He might have a name and address of a person, a mule, in the US to accept the funds, who will then be able to deliver the sum to the scammer, who's probably in a foreign country. He might ask you to buy I-Tune cards or gift cards. Then send him a photo of the back of the card after you scratch it off and reveal the code. They trade these for cash.

21. A scammer will probably send you love letters he copies and pastes from websites:

22. A scammer doesn't want you to tell your friends or family about him. He fears being exposed.

23. A scammer from Nigeria will have words out of order in his writing, there are 250 tribes in Nigeria with 521 languages and dialects. They sometimes speak in pidgen English.

24. The scammer is probably very young, so he might tease you, "I'll keep you young."

25. The scammer believes you have money if you've traveled a lot, if you have a successful job, if you don't have children around anymore, you own your home, or live alone.

26. He blames others for the troubles in his life and works hard to get your sympathy.

27. A scammer is intensely interested in you 100% of the time until he gets money, then about half that time. When you won't send any more money, then he is intensely interested again. Maybe you will

take out a loan, he figures? If the scammer can't get money from you, he might pass you on to a professional scammer.

28. A scammer's text might use someone's name other than yours or use "him" when it should be "her" because initially it was for another person. He cut and pasted and not proofread first.

29. There might be lapses in conversation. It could be because he's chatting with another woman or looking something up he doesn't have an answer for.

30. He might send the same message two or more times in a row. It could be because he's copying and pasting, and he hits the send button more than once.

31. If he calls you, you may have difficulty understanding him because of his accent or loud background noise. For example, one night, I heard a dog barking. My guy advised he was on his balcony, and a lady was walking her dog. It's difficult for the scammers to have any privacy, so they make excuses for the noise.

32. He is a master at making you feel guilty. "If you love me, you will help me." He might become verbally abusive if you refuse. Or, he might use reverse psychology. "If you don't want to help me, that's fine, but know I will always love you no matter what."

33. He may suggest having a sexual conversation.

34. He might tell you he had a sweet dream about you and describe it to you.

35. He may want your address to send you something. For example, my boyfriend sent me a stolen car to store in my driveway until he got home.

SCAMMERS OPERATIONS

Scammers are organized, work together, and share resources. This list describes the jobs.

Researchers – This person will locate photos of a person on Facebook, LinkedIn, dating sites, and blogs and create a profile. They train one or more to act as the contact person. You might see the same profile for a different man, as they're proficient at copying and pasting. Their victims tend to be lonely, romantic women. They come from small towns or rural areas, as they believe these women are trusting and hospitable and less informed about technology. The scammers focus on people living in Southern states and the Midwest, as they find these people fall for scams easier.

Writers – These people write longer letters and even give the contact person a list of phrases to use to keep the woman interested, engaged, and finally falling in love. I found similarly written letters on websites, so all they had to do was copy and paste.

Contact person – This person talks to the victim. He's been instructed on what phrases to use and possibly how to change his accent. He knows the names of her family members, pet's names, how her house was arranged, i.e., bedroom upstairs, and what she did on a regular day. He is efficient at detecting any emotion in her voice to respond appropriately. When he gets many responses on the dating site from his "perfect model photos," he weeds them out by ignoring those with one-word responses and then convinces the chosen ones to move off the dating website. Steve Cryer was my contact person.

Crier – This is obvious. This is who I'm sure was on the phone the first time I talked to Steve. He was frantic, maybe high on drugs or just a good actor.

Money manager – This person may be the "Boss" and the highest-paid member of the team. He receives the money from people like me, divides it up, keeps a small percentage, and transfers it to the Big Boss.

HIERARCHY IN SCAMMER TEAMS

They call it a "Money Game," not scamming. Some scammers have said they know it's wrong, but there's no shame in it. It's reparation for them being poor and taken advantage of.

Beginners – called "guy" or "G" – He asks for small money, maybe a couple of hundred dollars, or he might pass you on to a more experienced guy, as he doesn't have the tools, like fictitious websites or documents or fake camera videos. A beginner has no money, so he uses cell phone data, so he doesn't have to pay for calls. He might ask for money to be sent directly to Ghana or Nigeria as he has no contacts (mules) to collect money and send it to him. He learns by shadowing another scammer, and he pays him for training. Next, he learns what time of day is best to throw the bait out and on what platform. Finally, he learns how much time to allow before checking back with the client. Scammers spend up to 16 hours a day online seven days a week.

Small money – also called "guy" or "G" – He asks for a couple hundred or maybe $1,000. He has no tools. He might have a fictitious passport, or he may send you a cheap bouquet of flowers. Maybe he has "pickers" or "shore guys" or "mules" to pick up the money in the US or UK and keeps 10-20%, but sends the rest to the Big Boss.

Professional – also called "guy," "G," or "Boss" – He works for big money. He asks for thousands or millions of dollars. He knows how to use fictitious news, banking, websites, fake camera videos, passports, fake checks, contracts, certificates of marriage, and death certificates. He has access to hacked bank cards, so what he sends you will be expensive. It may be flowers, jewelry, or money if he sends you anything. But he's usually at the top of his game and makes very few mistakes. He won't mention Nigeria, but maybe South Africa, Dubai, the UK, Yemen, South America, or some other parts of the world where he says he travels.

Boss or Chair (Chairman) – He plays for real big money. He receives money almost every day from his lower-level Yahoo Boys or guys. He may live in the US, the UK, Malaysia, China or Egypt, or any other place with advanced internet, but usually not Nigeria or Ghana. He has ample information and resources such as software and things nobody else has. Many of these resources are restricted in Nigeria and require face-to-face contact, which increases the chances of being caught and traced. He has a bank account capable of handling large sums of money without questions. When a Yahoo Boy or "guy" does an advanced-fee-scam for big money, that money is sent to the "chair," who keeps 40% for himself. He is a good researcher and skilled on the internet. He knows how to break through security on dating sites. He has many skilled guys working for him. He lives a lifestyle of excess.

A Lexus Rx330 vehicle is the signature vehicle a man owns who's in the "trade." One Nigerian scammer shared in an interview, "As long as you don't visit the woman in her country and lose your home advantage, you're fine." (They're never coming to be with you!). Even an upright Nigerian police officer cannot return money from an already scammed person. It's gone! Nigerian scammers like to treat their girlfriends and impress others with lots of money they throw around. I saw a video of a young man standing on top of his car throwing out hundreds of US dollar bills and another guy walking through the streets throwing out money. I've read they like to bathe in expensive champagne, and at parties or clubs, they pour bottles of champagne over each other's heads. They're rich enough to throw away money, or at least they want others to believe they can.

PREPARE TO DATE ONLINE SAFELY

Five Important Steps:

1. Know the red flags.

2. Set up an email address used exclusively for online dating. (i.e., Gmail or Hotmail)

3. Purchase a burner phone and use it exclusively. This prevents others from determining your address.

4. Never give personal details: Last name, address, bank name and/or account information, credit card information, names of your family members.

5. Meet him in person in a public place asap, at least before he tells you, "I Love You."

To prepare your profile:

1. Don't share too much about yourself. Be mysterious, especially if you are widowed or retired. For example, write: "If I told you everything, what would we have to talk about?"

2. Don't say: "I'm new to online dating."

3. Don't say: "If you're a scammer, don't bother." This will attract a Professional scammer.

4. Be careful what photos you post, as one is fine. However, scammers look at how you dress or the background in the photo to determine your economic level. For example, I posted a photo of myself standing beside my new sports car. It wasn't a good idea.

Beware:

1. If in his photo he looks like a model.

2. Of the absence of any photos on his profile page.

3. If his occupation is: engineering, construction, oil drilling, geology, business, or anything that requires a lot of traveling.

4. If he says he's new to online dating.

5. If he says only positive things about himself, including how successful he's been and he has money.

6. If he uses poor grammar and punctuation. One example is: he might type "know" for "now." Or he might not capitalize "I."

7. If he has a grandiose life story, and there's constant drama.

8. If he travels for business or an investment opportunity very soon after chatting with him. Or if he can talk/text all hours of the day and night and for extended periods of time.

9. If he has excuse after excuse why he can't meet you in person.

10. If he has a child in school in a different country, or he's not able to care for his child and grandparents or other family members care for them.

COURT CASES

I received a phone call on August 13, 2019, from Patrick Swayze, Intelligence Specialist, in the U.S. Attorney's Office, in Charleston, West Virginia.

He stated he was investigating a woman in West Virginia who'd been involved in a fraud case, and my name came up, because of the report my daughter had made on the FBI-IC3 website. I had transferred money to Patricia D'Angelo for Steve Cryer. I learned from Mr. Swayze that she was a bank employee and had been laundering money, hundreds of thousands, and getting paid thousands to do so. He told me she was caught, and he wanted to know if I would agree to be a witness in her trial.

At first, I was leery of him. I'd been told so many lies by so many people. So, I called the office number he'd given me, and yes, he was a legitimate government employee of the U.S. Attorney's Office in West Virginia. So, this was just the beginning of our many conversations and correspondence with the officer and his staff. Mr. Swayze listened intently as I shared with him all the transactions I'd made, and then he asked for copies of receipts, of which I mailed. After I told him my history with Steve Cryer, he said I'd be a helpful witness in Patricia D'Angelo's trial, and possibly, but probably not, I could get some of my money returned. Would I be interested in telling my story in court? I told him I would.

This sixty-year-old woman was being held accountable for the transactions she'd made for a man she thought she was helping. Mr. Swayze told me Patricia D'Angelo was a married woman who'd met Lucas on a social media site. (Apparently Lucas and Steve Cryer were the same person) He wasn't able to reveal anything more about their relationship. But, even when the officer visited her several times in her home, she wouldn't be convinced he was lying to her. She wouldn't end the relationship with him, even when she was looking at possible jail time. I wanted to jump on a plane and go to her, try to convince her to stop this behavior, but I wasn't allowed to talk to her. I'd be allowed in the courtroom, if it went that far. Due to Covid, her case was postponed several times. But, she's in real trouble. My heart goes out to her.

POSTED IN
W. VIRGINIA – SOUTHERN DISTRICT

Huntington Woman Pleads Guilty to Role in
Nigerian Fraud Scheme | USAO-SDWV
JANUARY 11, 2022

HUNTINGTON, W.Va. — A Huntington woman pleaded guilty today in connection with her role as a money mule in a Nigerian fraud scheme that scammed money from individuals, many of whom were elderly.

According to court documents and statements made during the plea hearing, Patricia D'Angelo, 69, acted as a money mule for a Nigerian scammer. In May 2018, D'Angelo met "Lucas" online and although they never actually met in person, Dudding and Lucas communicated frequently by email and text messages.

D'Angelo set up numerous bank accounts in her name at several different banks that she would use to wire and receive fraudulent funds. D'Angelo received numerous deposits in those bank accounts from individuals located in the United States and abroad. She, and unnamed co-conspirators, would then transfer these funds to bank accounts located in Nigeria. To further the scheme, D'Angelo admittedly would make false and fraudulent representations to the financial institutions to make it appear that the wire transfers were being sent for legitimate purposes. On April 26, 2019, D'Angelo sent a wire transfer of $39,000 from her account to an individual in Montana. Upon questioning by a bank employee, D'Angelo lied about the wire transfer to aid Lucas in completing the transfer of funds to the designated recipient in Montana.

Over the course of the scheme, D'Angelo withdrew victim funds for her personal benefit. D'Angelo used the funds to pay her utility bills, satellite television service, groceries, drug store purchases, gasoline purchases, department store purchases, restaurants and took numerous cash withdrawals.

D'Angelo pleaded guilty to aiding and abetting an unlawful monetary transaction and faces up to 10 years in prison when she is sentenced on April 25, 2022. As part of her plea agreement, D'Angelo has agreed to pay $1,788,589.24 in restitution.

United States Attorney Will Billings made the announcement and commended the investigative work of the United States Secret Service, the Federal Deposit Insurance Corporation (FDIC) – Office of Inspector General and the South Charleston Police Department conducted the investigation.

***

I received a phone call in May of 2019, from the U.S. Treasury Department Office in Phoenix, Arizona. They were investigating Seth Asamoah Jnr. in a fraud case, and my bank transfer to him was discovered. The officer asked me if that was true, and what did I know about Mr. Asamoah.

The officer and I chatted that one time, and I told him my story, stating I had sent the man a lot of money, including the one transaction he referenced. He said this was an extensive case and that he may request more documentation at a later date. I didn't need to send him anything at that time, and I was not under investigation.

***

Both of these cases were the result of reports made to the FBI Internet Crime Complaint Center – IC3.

THE END

ACKNOWLEDGEMENTS

To my writing group. I wouldn't have been able to complete this project without your guidance, feedback and encouragement. I have learned so much from all of you. Special thanks to Jeanie H. and Brenda H. for editing, Allison for the cover formatting and Jennifer for formatting the document and getting it ready for print.

If you enjoyed reading

Rising From Deception

Please post your review on Amazon

For more information about the author
and this book please email her at
janetmarshall2930@gmail.com